Learning through Dramatics:
Ideas for Teachers and Librarians

Edited by Nancy Hanks Brizendine
and James L. Thomas

D1365233

ORYX PRESS
1982

The rare Arabian Oryx is believed to have inspired the myth of the unicorn. This desert antelope became virtually extinct in the early 1960s. At that time several groups of international conservationists arranged to have 9 animals sent to the Phoenix Zoo to be the nucleus of a captive breeding herd. Today the Oryx population is nearing 300 and herds have been returned to reserves in Israel, Jordan, and Oman.

Copyright © 1982 by The Oryx Press
2214 North Central at Encanto
Phoenix, AZ 85004

Published simultaneously in Canada

Printed and Bound in the United States of America

Library of Congress Cataloging in Publication Data
Main entry under title:

Learning through dramatics.

Bibliography: p.
Includes index.
1. Drama in education—Addresses, essays, lectures.   I. Brizendine, Nancy Hanks, 1946–
II. Thomas, James L., 1945–
PN3171.L37   371.3'32   82-2239
ISBN 0-89774-005-X   AACR2

Contents

Preface

Educators continually strive to identify new techniques to motivate and to interest students in the learning process. In today's media-aware world, teachers have found that they must use more than repetitive exercises to hold the attention of children and young adults. The use of dramatics offers an additional opportunity to aid, enhance, and reinforce the learning experience for all students.

Dramatization offers the teacher a unique opportunity to observe the individuals within a class and to learn their varied interests. This insight allows the teacher to design activities tailored to the needs of individuals or specific groups and to provide a learning situation in which students will succeed. By allowing students to utilize their own abilities, both intellectual and creative, and by making learning pleasurable, the educator will bring new excitement to the classroom or media center through dramatics. For those working with exceptional children, the need to relate to all areas of potential growth is essential. Dramatization provides a bridge of relevance to the curriculum and encourages participation across possible communication barriers. The librarian/media specialist will find a variety of ways to use dramatics to develop and enrich the programing of the media center.

The use of dramatics was once confined to the areas of language arts and English. Today, however, as evidenced in the literature, dramatization spans the curriculum, and its utilization in many fields reveals its usefulness and effectiveness as an instructional tool. *Learning through Dramatics: Ideas for Teachers and Librarians* provides examples of dramatization not only in the traditional subject areas, but also in social studies, science, reading, literature, career education, values, environmental studies, nutrition, creative writing, and vocabulary development. This compilation is intended for use by teachers of kindergarten through the 12th grade, teachers of exceptional children, and librarians/media specialists.

The articles chosen for this book were selected using the following criteria: (1) *practicality*—the articles are related expressly to a subject area and reflect a useful rather than a predominantly theoretical premise; (2)

authority—the authors are experienced individuals whose qualifications are listed in the contributors section of this book; (3) *recency*—the articles have been published within the last 10 years; and (4) *replication*—the articles provide techniques which can be utilized in a classroom or library/ media center setting.

Nancy Hanks Brizendine
James L. Thomas

Contributors

Dennis L. Allen, who formerly taught fifth grade, is an elementary school principal in North Olmsted, Ohio and the coauthor, with Robert J. Corey, of "Will the Mystery Guests Please Sign In?" Reprinted from *Teacher,* January 1977. Copyright © 1977 by Macmillan Professional Magazines. Used by permission of The Instructor Publications, Inc.

Eugene L. Aronin is Assistant Professor of Early Childhood at Texas Tech University, College of Education, Lubbock. "Creative Dramatics for Teaching Career Concepts to the Young Child" by Thomas D. Yawkey and Eugene L. Aronin originally appeared in *Elementary English* (January 1974, vol. 51, pp. 38–40, 44). Copyright © 1974 by the National Council of Teachers of English. Reprinted with permission.

Alfred A. Arth is Professor of Education, Department of Curriculum and Instruction, University of Wyoming, Laramie. "Dramatization and Gaming for Optimum Environmental Survival" by Alfred A. Arth and J. Howard Johnston originally appeared in *Elementary English* (April 1973, vol. 50, pp. 539–43). Copyright © 1973 by the National Council of Teachers of English. Reprinted with permission.

Violet Asmuth is a speech instructor at Edison Community College in Fort Myers, Florida. "Two Hits with One Throw: Drama and Values" originally appeared in the *English Journal* (February 1978, vol. 67, pp. 61–63). Copyright © 1978 by the National Council of Teachers of English. Reprinted with permission.

Edward Berry is the author of "Dramatic Steps into History." Reprinted from *Teacher,* December 1976. Copyright © 1976 by Macmillan Professional Magazines. Used by permission of The Instructor Publications, Inc.

Celestine Bloomfield is State Consultant, Division of Instructional Media, Indiana Department of Public Instruction, Indianapolis and the author of "The Media Specialist and Dramatic Productions." Reprinted from *Hoosier School Libraries*, 17 (February 1978): pp. 43–44 with the permission of the Association of Indiana Media Educators.

Libby Colman is coauthor of several books on child-bearing and is psychological assistant in a private psychiatric practice. She directs plays for the Sausalito School District in California and is author of ''Shakespeare for the Fun of It.'' Reprinted from INSTRUCTOR, November 1974. Copyright © 1974 by The Instructor Publications, Inc. Used by permission.

Elwanda Lu Conley is a vocational home economics teacher at Chapmanville Junior High School, West Virginia. ''How I Teach Nutrition'' is reprinted by permission from *Forecast for Home Economics* (September 1974, vol. 20, pp. 116, 120). Copyright © 1974 Scholastic Magazines, Inc. All rights reserved.

Robert J. Corey is a fifth-grade teacher at Glendale Elementary School, Bedford, Ohio and the coauthor, with Dennis L. Allen, of ''Will the Mystery Guests Please Sign In?'' Reprinted from *Teacher*, January 1977. Copyright © 1977 by Macmillan Professional Magazines. Used by permission of The Instructor Publications, Inc.

Barbara Blakely Duffelmeyer is an English, Spanish, and reading teacher at Bondurant-Farrar Junior-Senior High School in Bondurant, Iowa. ''Developing Vocabulary through Dramatization'' by Frederick A. Duffelmeyer and Barbara Blakely Duffelmeyer originally appeared in the *Journal of Reading* (November 1979, vol. 23, pp. 141–43). Reprinted with permission of Frederick A. Duffelmeyer, Barbara Blakely Duffelmeyer, and the International Reading Association.

Frederick A. Duffelmeyer is Assistant Professor of Elementary Education, Iowa State University, Ames. ''Developing Vocabulary through Dramatization'' by Frederick A. Duffelmeyer and Barbara Blakely Duffelmeyer originally appeared in the *Journal of Reading* (November 1979, vol. 23, pp. 141–43). Reprinted with permission of Frederick A. Duffelmeyer, Barbara Blakely Duffelmeyer, and the International Reading Association.

Margaret Egan is an English teacher of literature and composition, Notre Dame Academy, Staten Island, New York. ''A Primer of Drama Techniques for Teaching Literature'' by Catherine O'Shea and Margaret Egan originally appeared in the *English Journal* (February 1978, vol. 67, pp. 51–55). Copyright © 1978 by the National Council of Teachers of English. Reprinted with permission.

Rose M. Feinberg, Ed.D., is Director of Language Arts, Lunenberg Public Schools, Lunenburg, Massachusetts and the author of ''Acting Out Language Skills.'' Reprinted from INSTRUCTOR, October 1976. Copyright © 1976 by The Instructor Publications, Inc. Used by permission.

Patrick Groff is Professor of Education, San Diego State University, California and the author of ''Readers Theatre by Children.'' Reprinted from *Elementary School Journal* by permission of The University of Chicago Press. Volume 79, Number 1, © 1978 by the University of Chicago.

Carole C. Huggins holds a bachelor's degree in theater from the University of Kansas and has done graduate work in children's drama at the University of Washington in Seattle. ''Creative Dramatics: A New Kind of Library Program'' is reprinted from *Virginia Librarian* (October 1974, vol. 29, pp. 10–11, 14). Printed by permission of the *Virginia Librarian,* Virginia Library Association.

J. Howard Johnston is Associate Professor and Assistant Dean for Graduate Studies in Education, University of Cincinnati, Ohio. ''Dramatization and Gaming for Optimum Environmental Survival'' by Alfred A. Arth and J. Howard Johnston originally appeared in *Elementary English* (April 1973, vol. 50, pp. 539–43). Copyright © 1973 by the National Council of Teachers of English. Reprinted with permission.

Eleanor A. Kelly is a music teacher at St. Ignatius Loyola Elementary School in New York, an elementary school consultant, and the coauthor with Katherine Y. B. Yao of ''Integrating Science with the Creative Arts in Career Education.'' Reproduced with permission from *Science and Children,* November, 1975. Copyright © 1975 by the National Science Teachers Association, 1742 Connecticut Avenue, N.W., Washington, D.C. 20009.

Stephen Koziol, Jr. is Associate Professor in teacher development at the University of Pittsburgh, Pennsylvania. ''Research on Creative Dramatics'' by Julie Massey and Stephen Koziol, Jr. originally appeared in *English Journal* (February 1978, vol. 67, pp. 92–95). Copyright © 1978 by the National Council of Teachers of English. Reprinted with permission.

Arlene Leff is a second-grade teacher, Waterford-Halfmoon U.F.S.D., Waterford, New York and a consultant for the Empire State Youth Theater Institute in Albany. ''Elementary School Creative Dramatics: Coming to Your Senses'' by Walter Sawyer and Arlene Leff was originally published as ''All the World's a Stage: Creative Dramatics as a Language Arts Tool'' in *Contemporary Education* (Fall 1979, vol. 51, pp. 40–42). Reprinted with the permission of the authors and Indiana State University.

Michael Malkin is Professor of Theatre, California Polytechnic State University, San Luis Obispo and coauthor, with Pamela Malkin, of ''Theater in the Classroom: Part I & Part II.'' Reprinted from *Teacher,*

November 1975; December 1975. Copyright © 1975 by Macmillan Professional Magazines. Used by permission of The Instructor Publications, Inc.

Pamela Malkin is an acting teacher with the Central Coast Children's Theater, San Luis Obispo, California and coauthor, with Michael Malkin, of "Theater in the Classroom: Part I & Part II." Reprinted from *Teacher,* November 1975; December 1975. Copyright © 1975 by Macmillan Professional Magazines. Used by permission of The Instructor Publications, Inc.

Julie Massey is an instructor in the Department of Education, Lake Forest College, Lake Forest, Illinois. "Research on Creative Dramatics" by Julie Massey and Stephen Koziol, Jr. originally appeared in *English Journal* (February 1978, vol. 67, pp. 92–95). Copyright © 1978 by the National Council of Teachers of English. Reprinted with permission.

Katherine B. Murphy, a former teacher, is a member of the Minnesota State Arts Board and the author of "On the Trail of Lewis and Clark." Reprinted from *Teacher,* December 1976. Copyright © 1976 by Macmillan Professional Magazines. Used by permission of The Instructor Publications, Inc.

Betty Lou Nixon teaches elementary education at Rutgers College of Rutgers University, New Brunswick, New Jersey.. "Imagine That!" is reprinted from *School and Community,* September 1979, with permission of the Missouri State Teachers Association.

Catherine O'Shea is Chairperson of the English Department, St. Jean Baptiste High School, New York, New York. "A Primer of Drama Techniques for Teaching Literature" by Catherine O'Shea and Margaret Egan originally appeared in the *English Journal* (February 1978, vol. 67, pp. 51–55). Copyright © 1978 by the National Council of Teachers of English. Reprinted with permission.

Bryna Paston is Bucks County Editor of "The Jewish Times," published weekly in Philadelphia, and a free-lance writer. "The Pied Piper's Magic Endures" is reprinted by permission from *American Education* (October 1979, vol. 15, pp. 12–15).

Richard Lee Ponting teaches at Dudley Senior High School in Greensboro, North Carolina. "Combining Physics and Drama" is reprinted with permission from *Physics Teacher* (October 1978, vol. 16, p. 482) © 1978 American Association of Physics Teachers.

Jonathan Potter is an English teacher and Director of the Gifted/Talented Drama Program in Camden, Maine. "Liven Up Your Student Dramatics with Commedia Dell' Arte" originally appeared in *Media & Methods* (September 1980, vol. 17, pp. 47–49). Reprinted with permission from the September 1980 issue of *Media & Methods*.

Milton Reiling is the author of "Ms. Green's Garden" which originally appeared in *Early Years* (January 1979, vol. 9, pp. 66–68). Reprinted with permission of the publisher, Allen Raymond, Inc., Darien, CT 06820. From the January 1979 issue of *Early Years*.

Ruth Beaumont Reuse is the author of "All It Takes Is a Little Incentive" which originally appeared in *Media & Methods* (March 1977, vol. 13, p. 59). Reprinted with permission from the March 1977 issue of *Media & Methods*.

Betty D. Roe is Professor of Education, Tennessee Technological University, Cookeville. "Creative Drama Builds Proficiency in Reading" by Elinor P. Ross and Betty D. Roe originally appeared in *Reading Teacher* (January 1977, vol. 30, pp. 383–87). Reprinted with permission of Elinor P. Ross, Betty D. Roe, and the International Reading Association.

Elinor P. Ross is Professor of Education, Tennessee Technological University, Cookeville. "Creative Drama Builds Proficiency in Reading" by Elinor P. Ross and Betty D. Roe originally appeared in *Reading Teacher* (January 1977, vol. 30, pp. 383–87). Reprinted with permission of Elinor P. Ross, Betty D. Roe, and the International Reading Association.

Walter Sawyer is Language Arts Coordinator, Waterford-Halfmoon U.F.S.D., Waterford, New York and a consultant for the Empire State Youth Theater Institute in Albany. "Elementary School Creative Dramatics: Coming to Your Senses" by Walter Sawyer and Arlene Leff was originally published as "All the World's a Stage: Creative Dramatics as a Language Arts Tool" in *Contemporary Education* (Fall 1979, vol. 51, pp. 40–42). Reprinted with the permission of the authors and Indiana State University.

Judith Schickedanz is Associate Professor in the School of Education, Boston University. " 'You Be the Doctor and I'll Be Sick': Preschoolers Learn the Language Arts through Play" originally appeared in *Language Arts* (September 1978, vol. 55, pp. 713–18). Copyright © 1978 by the National Council of Teachers of English. Reprinted with permission.

Sarah Yoder Scott is instructing part-time at Oxford, Pennsylvania as a teacher/tutor in the migrant education program and is the author of "Not on Every Bush." Reprinted from INSTRUCTOR, March 1973. Copyright © 1973 by The Instructor Publications, Inc. Used by permission.

Elaine Campbell Smith was with the Department of Theater at Florida State University, Tallahassee. "Drama and the Schools: A Symposium" originally appeared in *Elementary English* (February 1972, vol. 49, pp. 299–306). Copyright © 1972 by the National Council of Teachers of English. Reprinted with permission.

John Warren Stewig is Professor of Curriculum and Instruction, University of Wisconsin, Milwaukee. "Drama: Integral Part of the Language Arts" originally appeared in *Elementary English* (January 1974, vol. 51, pp. 66–71). Copyright © 1974 by the National Council of Teachers of English. Reprinted with permission.

Gail Cohen Taylor compiled the ERIC/RCS Report entitled "Creative Dramatics for Handicapped Children" for *Language Arts* (January 1979, vol. 57, pp. 92–97, 106). The material is in the public domain.

Elaine Hoffman Wagener is the author of "Drama: Key to History for the Visually Impaired Child" which originally appeared in *Education of the Visually Handicapped* (Summer 1977, vol. 9, pp. 45–47). Copyright © 1977 by Heldref Publications.

Gloria Jane Wallin is the author of "Fostering Moral Development through Creative Dramatics" which originally appeared in *Personnel and Guidance Journal* (May 1980, vol. 58, p. 630). Copyright © 1980 American Personnel and Guidance Association. Reprinted with permission.

Andrea Wertheimer is an English and reading teacher at Junior High School 54M, New York, New York. "Story Dramatization in the Reading Center" originally appeared in the *English Journal* (November 1974, vol. 63, pp. 85–87). Copyright © 1974 by the National Council of Teachers of English. Reprinted with permission.

Katherine Y. B. Yao is the coauthor, with Eleanor A. Kelly, of "Integrating Science with the Creative Arts in Career Education." Reproduced with permission from *Science and Children,* November, 1975. Copyright © 1975 by the National Science Teachers Association, 1742 Connecticut Avenue, N.W., Washington, D.C. 20009.

Thomas D. Yawkey is Associate Professor of Early Childhood and Director of Project P.I.A.G.E.T. at The Pennsylvania State University, University Park. "Creative Dramatics for Teaching Career Concepts to the Young Child" by Thomas D. Yawkey and Eugene L. Aronin originally appeared in *Elementary English* (January 1974, vol. 51, pp. 38–40, 44). Copyright © 1974 by the National Council of Teachers of English. Reprinted with permission.

PART I
Overview

Introductory Comments

In editing 3 papers that provide an encompassing view of the relationships between drama and education, Elaine Campbell Smith, in "Drama and the Schools: A Symposium," surveys various aspects of the scope, goals, and potential of school programs utilizing drama. "Imagine That!" by Betty Lou Nixon describes exercises to stimulate creativity with children of different ages and ability levels; she notes that "Art and music give a child a chance to make something. Drama gives a child a chance to be something."

Julie Massey and Stephen Koziol, Jr. review many of the studies relating to creative dramatics and language development, cognitive development, and attitude change in "Research on Creative Dramatics." Through their research, they provide a foundation upon which the reader can base expected outcomes of experiences in creative dramatics.

Drama and the Schools: A Symposium

Edited by Elaine Campbell Smith

INTRODUCTION

More and more, educators are becoming aware of drama as a valuable
teaching aid. This is not so much because drama can encompass within its
boundaries every facet of knowledge known to man, but that drama involves the participant and learning comes through involvement. The theory
that "a person cannot be taught; he can only be exposed to a learning
situation," comes to mind. If a child is interested, he will learn. If a child is
involved, he is interested. Drama encourages involvement, by direct participation (improvisation, role playing, pantomime, characterization) and
by indirect participation (emphatic responses to dramatic presentations).
Those seeking help to encourage the use of such dramatic processes can
turn to specialists. Many experts in the field of drama have concentrated
their creative efforts on developing methods by which drama can be utilized
as a basic tool in learning. What these experts have to offer is a better
understanding of the theories of drama and a more concrete realization of
the possibilities of drama in education.

Creative dramatics is sometimes used in the elementary grades as a
tool for learning. Most often, however, there is little or no use of drama as a
teaching aid in the secondary school. In a well-developed and inclusive
program of drama in schools, all grades—K through 12—would be introduced to learning through drama at levels compatible with learning skills at
those levels. The flow of learning is a continuous process and there is no
definite dividing line between elementary and secondary education. It is a
merging and maturing experience that should be viewed as a totality. The
work done in drama in the elementary grades should be followed through
with experiences in drama in the secondary grades.

The preceding topics were discussed in a symposium held at Florida
State University where various approaches to the use of drama in the

elementary and secondary schools were considered. The papers for this symposium were prepared by Dr. Moses Goldberg, Dr. Joseph Karioth, and Mr. Jon Spelman.

Dr. Goldberg is Director of Children's Drama at Florida State University and is head of the Children's Theatre, which annually tours throughout the state. He has written plays for children which have been produced. He currently teaches courses in acting, directing and children's theatre. Dr. Joseph Karioth is Head of the Professional Training program at Florida State University. He sponsors the ''Pied Pipers,'' a performing group for young children. He has acted and directed for the Tyrone Guthrie Theatre, directed for the Manitoba Theatre in Canada and acted in various television series. Jon Spelman is Director of Education at the Asolo, the State Theatre company located in Sarasota, Florida. He is in charge of the state-wide tour, which annually presents daylong enrichment programs to thousands of high school students.

The three papers follow the general topic of drama somewhat differently; however, they contain points of common agreement. The undeniable center of accordance is that drama is an important and enriching element for use in the learning and maturing process.

THEATRE IN EDUCATION: A SUMMARY OF BENEFITS

MOSES GOLDBERG

Communities where effective educational practices coexist with excellent theatrical artistry are few. If a viable theatre program could be thoroughly integrated with a liberalized school system, the gain might be viewed as significant for both the theatre artist and the educator. In parts of England, much of the Soviet Union, and isolated communities in other lands, one can occasionally find a ''theatre in education'' program. These programs are designed to increase the educational effectiveness of the school system and to contribute to the nurturance of a healthy artistic tradition in the community involved. The goals of such a program are aesthetic values, pedagogical values and psychological values.

Aesthetically, the theatre can bring much to the life of the child; much that he would not receive from any of the more traditional school subjects or even from music or art programs. The theatre is the only art form that deals with human behavior in a totally recognizable way. First, and most important, the theatre provides *enjoyment*. Without the heightened motivation and receptivity which accompany the child's total enjoyment of an experience, all subsequent values are weakened or even negated. Hence the artistry of the theatre production is of extreme importance. Once the highest level of audience entertainment is achieved, other aesthetic values follow.

Second, the theatre provides *expression*—the child's spontaneous emotional reaction to the play and the characters. This brings about *participation*—the action of helping to create the artistic event; for all the performing arts are temporal, and necessarily involve the audience of the moment as a part of the final aesthetic product. Finally, with a maturation of aesthetic sensibility, comes that paradoxical state which is the actual aesthetic experience. The individual in the audience *simultaneously identifies* with the onstage characters and actions, and yet disassociates himself from both. The child sits secure and safe, and yet undergoes soul-wrenching experiences indirectly. This vicarious experience has probably never been satisfactorily explained; but seems to hold the secret of the attractiveness of the arts for man. The vicarious experiences of a fictional life can lead to a purging of tensions—the Aristotelian ''catharsis''—or to an intellectual awareness of human potentialities and limits. Both of these reactions can be spiritually uplifting. Vicarious experience is the highest goal of all theatre and no doubt requires some audience sophistication. An experience, however, can be so intense that a person's life style can be dramatically changed by a single powerful aesthetic adventure. This can occur if the production is good enough and the components of identification are truly relevant to that individual's current self-image.

Pedagogically, the theatre can capitalize on the child's heightened motivation to indirectly inculcate facts and ideas. Direct teaching, it should be noted, often fails; it disrupts the aesthetic experience. The subtle introduction of significant material is among the most effective of all teaching methods. Four classes of information may be learned from plays.

1. The *content* of the play. A play set in Japan teaches Cultural Anthropology, whether it tries to or not. A play about Louis Pasteur cannot fail to teach French Culture, History, Science and Psychology—unless the play is so bad that the audience fails to attend to it.

2. The *conventions of the theatre*. Like all institutions, the theatre has special rules which govern its function. The use of a curtain and lights, the structure of a scene, the special ways of indicating the death of a character or the passing of time, and so forth, have conventional rules. By seeing these rules in action, the child absorbs them.

3. *Cultural learning*. A play by a modern American author conveys the thought processes and the cultural unconscious of modern America. By studying Greek plays, we understand not only the Greek customs revealed in the play, but also the ingrained cultural philosophy which the Greek adult audience was never aware of—and which we find ex-

tremely revealing. The child is a little bit like a foreigner who fails to grasp completely the way his adult environment thinks. The play subtly exposes him (as does literature) to cultural patterns of thought.

4. *Ethics*. The Judeo-Christian ethical code is at the base of most Western drama. The child can most quickly learn the particulars of "right" and "wrong" in his own culture from folklore and from theatre.

Psychologically, the theatre brings values to children that are twofold. Through role awareness and character identification, the child learns *socialization skills*. A single play allows him to know quite well half a dozen people he would not otherwise meet. To be able to empathize with others is the beginning of social intelligence. The theatre provides a golden opportunity to live in the shoes of another human being—again assuming that the artistic quality of the performance is sufficiently high. The other psychological value is the *personal maturation* of the child. By recognizing his own current psychological crisis in another, the child can be helped to see that the problem—whatever it is—can be solved. As he passes through crisis after crisis in roughly the same order along which man has always struggled up the path to self-knowledge and self-actualization, exposure to the right play at the right time perhaps eases his transitions.

All the values here outlined exist in developmental sequences. Some are most appropriate to the young child, others to the adolescent. The primary grade child experiences the most naive pleasures. His participation is blatant and functional. He learns the most basic conventions of the theatre, and how to distinguish theatre from television. His plays deal heavily with cultural and ethical learning—especially the fairy tales. His psychological crises typically involve choosing between acceptable and unacceptable behaviors—a "good" and an "evil."

In the intermediate grades the plays can become more sophisticated. At this level the child can express more complex emotions. His participation ranges from offering to help his hero, to laughing at the same hero's foibles. He is beginning to know how to achieve aesthetic distance. Pedagogically, he profits much from cultures other than his own. He learns the traditions of the theatre, and some of its historical styles. His cultural and ethical learning become more subtle, as his plays assume more and more that certain types—the braggart, for example—are laughable in our society. These assumptions become the child's lessons. Social awareness begins to become important as he learns to apply "good" and "evil" to role and situation. His crises of personality deal with peer acceptance and self-image much more than simply with doing what is "right."

The Junior High youth aspires to an adult level of entertainment. Most of these children are ready for a full aesthetic experience—even a tragic one. The child's participation becomes more internal and may even seem to be against the play's requirements if he feels the play's values are inconsistent or ineffectively portrayed. It is at this stage that the child can easily learn about conflicting life styles, about interpersonal and intra-personal conflicts, and about the relevance of the theatre experience to the evolution of his own self-concept. If he learns this latter lesson, his choice of arts will become a lifetime habit. Social intelligence becomes keenly critical to him now, as does the establishment of life goals. The theatre can help, especially when his childish goals are unrealistic, as is typical of this age.

The High School student, the young adult, is aesthetically sophisticated. He is able to criticize the aesthetic experience even while enjoying it. His pedagogical interests are in the classics (plays which form our theatre heritage) and in plays which are specifically about young adults. He begins to have definite preferences for theatrical forms, and even certain playwrights. Psychologically, he learns about significant lives—the life of Hamlet, for example, or of Dobie Gillis. He reaches out for full self-actualization—the existential creation of his own unique philosophy of life. He becomes, with the help of his aesthetic enrichment, a mature adult.

The theatre can be relevant to this maturation in many ways. The final product—the show—is not the only way. Dramatic process can also be made an integral part of the school program, providing a link between the aesthetic production and the everyday behavior of the child. Throughout, however, the theatre experience provides the dynamic focus for development. Aroused and challenged by good theatre, appropriately gauged to his maturational level, the child quickly learns to regard these experiences as among the most influential of his educational career. The more regularly they can be provided, and the more thoroughly they can be integrated into the total educational program, the greater the benefit.

DRAMA AND THE ELEMENTARY SCHOOL CHILD

JOSEPH KARIOTH

With the increasing demands by administrators, teachers, and parents to include drama activities as a regular part of the elementary school day, it seems appropriate to suggest certain behavior patterns that can be expected as a result of dramatic experience. Assuming a space in which to play, a group of children to play and a trained leader familiar with dramatic activities for children, the following developmental behavior patterns may be expected.

Impression Behavior

It is through the five senses that the child becomes aware of and learns about the world. All the information the child will ever receive comes through the senses and since information is the basis of skill acquisition, of attitude development, and of knowledge, it is absolutely essential that each child's senses are developed to the maximum. Through beginning sense exercises advancing to the more discriminating sense activities the dramatics leader is constantly helping the child to expand his sense awareness and consequently his understanding of the world.

Expression Behavior

As we breathe in, must we breathe out. As we are stimulated, must we respond. All responses are expressed through the use and control of voice and body. Not so long ago it was quite fashionable to talk about communication breakdown. Indeed today there are still those who refer to all human problems as communication breakdown when, in fact, if one examines the interaction situation, what probably is at fault is expression behavior breakdown. How many times has the child said, ''I don't know the word, I don't know what I feel, I don't know what I'm thinking''? If the child is thinking or if the child is feeling, he knows it—he simply can't express it. It is through the use of vocalization and physicalization activities that the leader starts the child on his way to successful expression behavior.

Communication Behavior

To communicate is to share thoughts or feelings. Articulation and inflectional skills, vocabulary building and language acquisition are all developed through dialogue activities. Pantomime teaches facial and body gestures. It is through the language of words and gestures that we communicate with each other.

Social Behavior

All human behavior may be ascribed to particular roles. The more behavior exhibited, the easier it is to identify the particular role. One easily recognizes a teacher, a policeman, or a doctor. Particular role behavior is always in relation to another role. Teacher behavior implies student behavior; doctor behavior implies patient behavior. It is the pattern of role relationships that constitutes a functioning social system; that is, the role relationships in that society are harmonious. If a society is disrupted it is because role relationships are unharmonious: An unharmonious role relationship is the case where the expected behavior does not occur. For example, the teacher does not expect the student to get up and walk out of the room when the teacher is discussing a particular topic. The patient does not expect the doctor to walk out of the operating room. It is when one is able to exhibit the expected role behavior in a role relationship that one has successful interaction; and it is interaction behavior that we refer to as social behavior. The dramatics leader utilizes role playing situations, socio-drama, improvisations, and scripted plays to impart an understanding and knowledge of the kinds of patterns of behavior that are expected in particular role relationships.

Creative Behavior

Creative behavior has been defined in as many ways as there are scholars in the field. But for our purposes let us say that the child is exhibiting creative behavior when he is (1) fluent, able to produce many ideas, (2) flexible, able to produce different categories of ideas, (3) original, able to produce new or different combinations of ideas, and (4) elaborate, able to embellish his ideas so that they become more provocative and evocative. In a very real sense it is creative behavior that defines one's individuality. In fact, a person's personality might well be defined in terms of his creative behavior. The entire spectrum of dramatic activities encourages the child to develop creative behavior characteristics. In planning the story, the scene, the setting, the character, the character's dialogue, his movement and his costuming and in executing the plans, the child is constantly in an atmosphere that allows and, indeed, demands creative behavior.

These four distinct behavior patterns will grow out of and be developed by a dramatics program with children. Within each behavior pattern there are certain skills that are acquired through dramatic activities; there are certain attitudes toward behavior patterns that are invoked by dramatic activities; and there is certain knowledge of and about each behavior pattern that becomes understood by participating in a dramatics program.

PROFESSIONAL THEATRE IN THE SCHOOLS

JON SPELMAN

In the last decade, the professional nonprofit theatre has come a long way in its relationships with the public schools. In the early 1960's, many people believed that all theatre was like the New York commercial theatre: organized as a business for the purpose of making a financial profit. In the mid sixties when non-profit theatres began performing for students, many people still believed that theatres were doing so only to provide employment for their actors and to make financial profit. But now, the legitimate educational concerns of many theatre troupes are widely recognized and another job has begun; defining and implementing the professional company's role in the education process.

There are some obvious tasks a professional theatre can accomplish for schools. The company's plays and its staff can introduce new ways of thinking about curriculum while providing the specific tool of a more stimulating and effective way of teaching dramatic literature. A program of fullscale quality productions of worthwhile plays should be supplemented by appearances of actors in the classrooms. On stage the actor is viewed as a character. In a classroom or a workshop, the actor can be viewed as a large, responsive, and highly trained visual aid. He can lead in-service training for teachers and present workshops for students aimed at explicating the language, the conventions, by which theatre communicates. In such a situation, the actor would not simply present plays, he would demonstrate how actors work in dramatic literature. He would present "literature through performance," read poetry, dramatize history. The actor should not only perform dramatic roles; he should take an active instructional role in the educational process by presenting specially designed performances, by integrating the performance experience to the educational experience, and by relating the artistic experience to the educational experience.

Seven basic "human resources" are used as tools for cognitive awareness and creative behavior: *concentration, the senses, imagination, the body, the voice, emotions* and *intellect*. All of these "resources" are simultaneously used as tools and evaluated as products at each of the commonly recognized three stages in a drama program; discovery of one's self (early primary level); discovery (or rediscovery) of the immediate environment (later primary); the relating to the larger environment (middle level). But a fourth stage, related to and growing out of the earlier three, must be recognized and should be included in the sequence of the secondary school drama program. The earlier experiences with the dramatic process result (at the secondary level) in the exploration of the process of theatrical creation by a means of permitting a full confrontation with the professionally-produced play. The professional theatre can promote a systematic contact between the secondary schools and the theatre companies and the two together can develop models for student and teacher experience of the art process under the guidance of the theatre professionals.

Drama in the schools is directly related to professional theatre and actors. The professional serves as a standard-bearer, a pacesetter, a model, and the provider of the most intense experiences of their kind. The following attitudes, shared by the educator and the new breed of theatre professional, determine the nature of the experiences provided by the professional actor-teacher:

1. Conditions appear to have favored the development of creativity in the elementary, but not the secondary schools. Very recently, this trend has begun to change.

2. There are illuminating similarities between the teacher-student relationship and the actor-audience relationship.

3. An actor has the same basic ''human resources'' as the student. Acting is an emotional response to imagined sensory impulses.

4. The actor is akin to the child; he ventilates emotions that can find no other adequate outlet. With the actors' aid, an audience of adolescents can experience this same freedom.

5. A professional theatre program can fulfill certain educational needs that can be met by no other activity.

6. Because performances are audience-centered, the performing company must be professional. Only the professional company is likely to have a sufficiently high level of skill acquisition to prevent the performance from being actor-centered. Actor-centered performance, like creative drama, should aim at developing people—at providing ''practice in living.''

7. Plays and actors' appearances in the classroom must always be, but never seem, educational. One of the great advantages to such a program lies in the enjoyment experienced by all parties.

8. Plays and actors display a great confidence in and an ability of articulate expression—a primary goal of education.

9. Education for social roles can capitalize on the enormous humanizing influence of the theatrical experience. To really see another person's point of view makes the student more free, more tolerant. The play is not concerned with similarities between people; it is the conflict between people that is the essence of the dramatic.

10. Plays demonstrate vivid attempts to answer questions. How do men and women get along? What is important about Abe Lincoln? What is immoral? These are three of numberless possible examples.

11. The aesthetic experience of theatre is a very complex feeling and the aesthetic response is probably too sophisticated to expect from most secondary students. *Instinctive* feelings, concerned with the practical values of experience, are more likely and probably more useful at this level than aesthetic responses. The theatre program should not be

designed for exclusively aesthetic reasons ("plays for their own sake").

12. Instinctive responses are emotional and sensory. Critical and analytic responses should grow organically out of the non-intellectual responses. Emotions and senses exist not for their own sakes, but for the practical ends toward which they urge us.

13. Most of an actor's success rests on how successfully he evokes association in the minds of the observer. The professional actor works primarily with the content of students' minds, rather than with the content of his own mind. Professional plays have the effect of increasing the perceptual and communicative skills of the audience.

14. In the cognitive area, play attendance is perhaps the best teacher of such concepts as *theme, sequence, structure, conflict, characterization* and *scene*.

15. Observation, concentration, and imagination are the essential tools of an audience member and the essential ingredients in creative thinking. Attendance at professional performances of plays, when supplemented by less conventional contact with professional actors, can be an extraordinary force in the development and maintenance of the flexibility and originality which characterize creative behavior.

SUMMARY

A common thread of agreement running through the three preceding papers is that drama can be a significant and fruitful component for use in education. Additionally, one notes that even with the varying approaches taken by Goldberg, Karioth, and Spelman, there are, nevertheless, other important commonalities. Human behavior and human potentialities come in for considerable discussion. In conjunction with this, interaction and communication are focal points and, essentially, all three writers indicate that drama can enlarge on and develop given potential in this area. As well, all three papers touch on the aesthetic, the imaginative, the creative wellsprings of drama.

The three papers differ in kind and scope by choice of the authors. Goldberg elects to paint the larger canvas by first providing broad goals for a "theatre in education" program. Such goals are seen in the categories of aesthetic values, pedagogical values and psychological values. The explicitness with which Goldberg covers these points provides much which could be of use to teachers and other school personnel. The short but well thought out statements concerning sequential development provide an added dimension.

Karioth emphasizes the importance of sensory modality and sense development in children. His discussion of communication and interaction from the progressive viewpoints of impression behavior, expression behavior, communication behavior and social behavior culminates in his final discussion of creative behavior. In this paper much of the theory concerning drama and the elementary child is covered briefly but well, so that the analysis contains not only a sound base but also practical consideration for which the classroom teacher is often looking.

In the third paper, the professional theatre and its relationship to the schools is discussed. The beginnings of this relationship and the evolving of it from a legitimate educational concern to a fullscale educational enterprise indicates the degree to which schools are now turning to drama to provide a multitude of educational solutions. Spelman discusses the use of "human resources" and the capacity of theatre to use these resources as "tools for cognitive awareness and creative behavior." And here, as in the other papers, imagination comes in for its share of the discussion, not only in the actor-audience relationship but in the teacher-student interaction as well.

The papers individually represent an overall and broad view of drama and education, a discussion of dramatic activities with children, and the wide range of human resources professional theatre makes available to schools. In this respect, the three papers make for a rather total look at a survey of drama and the schools as viewed by specialists in this area. And in this comprehensive symposium, one readily sees why more and more the schools are turning to drama for a new look at learning.

Imagine That!

by Betty Lou Nixon

In a TV-oriented society such as ours, creative dramatics can help the teacher encourage the child to think, express himself, release emotions, understand feelings, develop confidence and get to know himself.

For the gifted child, drama can nurture creativity. For the under-privileged child, drama can serve as a stimulant to senses. The special child can dramatize his fears, frustrations, his anger or his lack of understanding. He can learn to cope and accept and even be proud of his differences. For the normal and special child to dramatize together can mean relaxation, security, or just fun. Drama is an essential part of education of all people of different abilities and ages.

Children in the primary grades are endowed with a most vivid and creative imagination. They especially need their teacher to create a classroom environment that encourages them to feel accepted and to contribute something to the dramatic experience.

The teacher must provide the area or space in which the drama can take place, the opportunity for the child to explore and the necessary materials to create and implement their ideas. As long as the materials are simple, bright and colorful, almost anything is suitable for working with the primary-grade child in creative dramatics. In fact, props are not always necessary. To be really creative, props should be imaginary. Just a child's creative mind is enough so long as the activity is related to the time and the child.

Consider the following ideas for a time to create, a time to dramatize:

- Dramatize man landing on the moon. Use electronic music for background and atmosphere.
- Dramatize life under the ocean.
- Use drama to show the rotation patterns of the sun, moon and earth.
- Dramatize the changing seasons.
- Study plants and act out their relationship to one another.
- Play stockbrokers—set up stocks, brokerage house and learn about Wall Street.

- Recreate and act out historical events.
- Role-play professions—their place in the community and services offered.
- Take time every day to communicate without speaking (pantomime).
- Create Disney World from cardboard cartons. Act out characters.
- Act out problems and future roles of the child.
- Use drama to learn to follow directions.
- Dramatize a painting, movie, song or favorite character.
- Dramatize social courtesies, manners.
- Use role reversal for understanding minority cultures.
- Enact something good that has happened to you and something bad.
- Use puppets to let children participate with musical pitch, expression and tempo.
- Have the group act as a train; movement awareness is the result.
- Use movement to show rhythm and dexterity. How many ways can you walk across a room?
- Tell movement stories. Act as "body machines," showing emotions with different body parts.
- Use words to symbolize *happy, sad, tired, hungry* in "word machines," where each person says a word to match his movement or feeling.
- Give the children a list of unknown vocabulary words. Have them look up meanings and act out the words as part of a sentence.

Through such creative experiences, an event comes to life. Art and music give a child a chance to make something. Drama gives a child a chance to be something.

By actually "being" something the child may understand much better a concept that the teacher may later verbalize. Children remember things that they do physically!

Creative dramatics may be taught as an end or as a tool. Whatever the case, drama can meet the needs of every child. It should be recognized as an essential aspect of the school curriculum. Through creative dramatic experience the child will learn to manipulate, explore and develop a certain degree of readiness for future endeavors. Drama has a way of making a child feel good about himself and his school.

Research on Creative Dramatics

by Julie Massey and Stephen Koziol, Jr.

As is evident in these statements from the report of the Arts, Education, and Americans Panel chaired by David Rockefeller, Jr., there are conflicting perspectives on the future of the arts, including creative dramatics, in school programs generally and in the English classroom in particular. Creative dramatics advocates proclaim a myriad of worthwhile outcomes from students' participation in creative dramatics activities including ''wholesome emotional development,'' ''inner security,'' ''social cooperation,'' ''creative expression,'' ''critical thinking,'' ''concentration,'' ''physical poise,'' ''sensory awareness,'' ''basic skills,'' ''aesthetic sensibility,'' and on and on. Skeptics about the value of creative dramatics and proponents of other orientations (e.g., basic skills or ''fundamentals'' advocates), however, have repeatedly noted the paucity of empirical evidence to support such claims. While there is certainly need to enlarge the research base in creative dramatics, there is also need to clarify just what the existing research has shown.

As we proceeded with our review of studies in creative dramatics, several problems became apparent. Foremost was the difficulty of determining just what individual researchers meant when they used such terms as roleplaying, improvisation, creative dramatics, warm-up, role-taking, and socio-drama among others. These terms were used in obviously different ways by different researchers and too few provided sufficient detail to allow the reader a clear sense of exactly what was done. Related problems included ambiguity about the context in which the creative dramatics activities took place and no consistency in the delineating of the role of the teacher or in the sequencing of different activities. In some studies, the creative dramatics activities were carried out in the classroom; in others, they were carried out in other environments. In some studies, the creative dramatics work was directly tied to the existing curriculum; in others, it was an adjunct. In some studies, the classroom teacher implemented the activities (sometimes with training and sometimes without); in others, leadership for the activities was provided by an outsider (usually the researcher). In some studies, the creative dramatics leader was an active agent in instruction; in others, that individual had a very passive role. In some studies, creative dramatics meant one isolated experience (sometimes as short as twenty minutes); in others, it meant a sequence of activities extending over one, or two, or three months.

All of these problems may very well be traced to the very breadth of the claims made by the creative dramatics advocates. With no clear limit on the nature of the expected outcomes, there has been little unity among researchers on what outcomes are most important or on how change and progress are to be measured. Unlike researchers in such areas as response to literature, composing, and language development, groups of researchers in creative dramatics have reached no consensus about what constitutes the focus of their work or on what measures should be used to identify changes in students' knowledge, skills, or attitudes and values. As a result, it is difficult to find substantial evidence in support of any specific claim, or on the use of any specific set of activities, or on consistent student change as determined through use of a specific set of measures.

In order to provide some structure to our discussion, we decided to consider findings as they related to only three major areas: language development; cognitive development including content comprehension and retention; and attitude change and appreciation. Although this decision meant that some studies would be excluded, it seemed to us the "best fit" for the majority of available studies in creative dramatics, especially in relation to work in the middle school and secondary school English classroom.

CREATIVE DRAMATICS AND LANGUAGE DEVELOPMENT

In response to the demand for more evidence of the positive effects of experiences in creative dramatics, many researchers have focused attention on a variety of dimensions in language development. Not surprisingly, there is great diversity in the nature of the studies with some dealing explicitly with the use of creative dramatics exercises to accomplish very concrete "language development" goals and others employing language growth or language fluency measures among an array of general measures.

Illustrative of the former is Fitzsimmons' (1975) study of vocabulary learning and retention with ninth grade students. Students in one group played with teacher-designated vocabulary words over a five week period using a variety of what were primarily sound and movement exercises. Students in another group "played" with the words using a variety of written exercises including sentence completion and group story writing, while students in a third group alternated between the creative dramatics and the writing methods. Results showed no significant differences among the groups on the weekly recall tests, but did show a significant difference in favor of the creative dramatics group on a retention test given after the treatment period.

Knudson (1971), on the other hand, included several language variables as part of his study of his "Specialized Language Activities Program" with below average ability rural ninth grade students. As a major part of this program, students working in small groups selected "problems," researched information related to the problem, developed scripts for a play using improvisation and feedback, and finally performed their play for videotape. Results showed that students participating in the experimental program for a year demonstrated significantly greater improvement than a comparison group on a variety of language dimensions including reading comprehension, use of Standard English, writing complexity as well as oral fluency.

Ridel (1975) worked with "regular" ninth grade students using a creative dramatics program based on Spolin's *Improvisation for the Theatre* (1963) on a once per week basis for an entire semester. On the basis of ratings given by selected teachers making independent judgments of pre- and posttest writing samples, Ridel concluded that the exposure to the Spolin activities over the semester had a positive effect on students' writing abilities.

Other researchers have generally found similar results. Lowke (1975), for example, found improvement in the use of "expressive" language by tenth graders working with literature using choral reading and sound/movement warm-up exercises. Rice (1971) found that kindergarten children participating in a program including a heavy "creative dramatics" component and taught by teachers with inservice training in dramatics showed significant growth in visual and auditory language skills as well as positive gains in vocabulary concepts. In a therapeutic setting, Irwin, Levy, and Shapiro (1972) found significant growth in verbal fluency by children involved in drama therapy. Hendrickson and Gallegos (1972) observed that elementary age Mexican-American children involved in a program wherein they worked with real-life situations using sound/movement exercises, pantomime, improvisation, and roleplay showed significantly greater improvement in language skills than did a comparison group who simply discussed the situations. Similarly, Strickland (1973) found that a six-month literature-oral language-dramatics program succeeded in helping two groups of Black kindergarteners to *expand* their "language repertoire" to include Standard English.

All of these studies suggest that the long term and consistent use of creative dramatic activities can have positive impact on the oral and written language abilities of children of widely different ages, with different ''academic'' abilities, and from diverse ethnic and cultural backgrounds.

CREATIVE DRAMATICS AND COGNITIVE DEVELOPMENT

As in the case with language development, researchers on the relationship between creative dramatics and cognitive development have tended either to concentrate on generalized cognitive skills or on specifics of content recall, retention, or analysis. In a recently completed study, Cercone (1976) considered the impact of a twelve week dramatic activity program both on general critical thinking abilities (Watson-Glaser Critical Thinking Appraisal) and on content knowledge and understanding based on carefully constructed literature tests. As part of the program, one group of tenth graders participated in a sequence of small group improvisations carefully designed to parallel situations in the literature that the students were reading while the second group participated in a similar sequence but with stimulus situations not directly related to the literature. Cercone concluded that both groups made marked gains on the critical thinking test and that, while there were no significant differences between the groups on the content-specific tests, the ''parallel situation'' group seemed to exhibit better overall comprehension of the literature.

Salvo (1972) and Macaluso (1973) both conducted studies to compare the literature comprehension of high school students engaged in a performance-oriented curriculum with that of similar students in a discussion-oriented one. Salvo (1972) worked with two groups of eleventh graders engaged in the study of *Our Town*. Under his direction, one group spent three weeks preparing and finally producing the play in their class while the other group participated in the interpretive-analytical study of the play through class discussions. On a standardized ''comprehension'' test for the play, students in the performance-oriented group demonstrated significantly superior comprehension immediately after the unit was completed, on a first retention test given three weeks later, and on a second retention test given three weeks after that.

Macaluso (1973) dealt with the study of Albee's *The American Dream* and *The Sandbox* by eleventh grade students over a seven day period. All students read on their own and then took a comprehension test on the first play. Students in one group then studied the second play using an analytic-discussion method while those in a second group were asked to prepare a production of the play. Both groups showed significantly better comprehension of the second play but there was no significant difference between the two groups. Similar results in comprehension and retention are reported by Lowke (1975) in her very brief study with tenth graders. Ingersoll and Kase (1971), in a carefully designed but very brief study of literature comprehension and retention with fifth and sixth grade children, found that creative dramatics activities generally had a positive influence on learning and retention. However, when students who had little prior experience with such work were taught lessons using creative dramatics, male students' retention was adversely affected while female students benefited. The authors suggest that girls in that age group are in general more accustomed to "acting out" and thus more comfortable with it than similar age boys.

On the basis of these studies, it would seem that work in creative dramatics can be a positive influence on cognitive development generally and on the comprehension and retention of literature. At the very least, such activities clearly do not detract from students' performance on conventional literature comprehension objective measures.

CREATIVE DRAMATICS AND ATTITUDE CHANGE

Many of the studies dealing with creative dramatics and language development or cognitive development have included consideration of students' attitudes toward the activities or toward English, and/or their appreciation and enjoyment of literature. Ridel (1975), for example, found that, while her ninth grade students' response showed an increased enthusiasm for drama, they had not changed in their attitudes toward English. Brandes (1971), in a study using creative dramatics to influence attitudes toward bidialectalism, found that girls tended to have the most positive attitudes, while college age students had a less favorable response toward bidialectalism than did high school students. McCaffrey (1973) reported that an "oral-dramatic method" used to teach poetry over four weeks to low-ability tenth and twelfth grade students resulted in an improvement in class involvement and in the appreciation of poetry but no change in the student's expressed attitudes toward poetry.

As part of his work with rural ninth graders, Knudson (1971) also considered aspects of his students' affective behavior. He reported that students expressed and demonstrated positive improvement in their attitudes toward their peers, their families, their community, and themselves. He also noted students' reactions extended to improve attendance and grooming.

Ruttle (1975) used two instruments, one a Likert-type test to measure students' attitudes toward their seventh grade Language Arts class, and one an ''Attitudes Towards Dramatics'' test (modeled after an earlier version by Hoetker and Robb) to determine changes in students' attitudes after a nine week experience which included about six hours of creative dramatics. While her students expressed very positive attitudes about the nine week curriculum as a whole, they did not show any appreciable change in their attitudes toward dramatics.

Cercone's (1976) study with tenth graders is also very important here because it begins to make distinctions between a creative dramatics program carried out in a direct curricular context and one carried out in the English classroom without that connection. Like Ruttle, she also used two sets of attitude instruments and found that both groups expressed more favorable attitudes toward reading and studying literature as a result of the twelve-week treatment period. The only area in which the two groups showed any significant difference was in the extent to which they perceived the curricular value of creative dramatics. Both groups expressed enjoyment about the activities and a desire to continue with them, but the direct context group expressed much greater perception that the activities also contributed substantially to their learning.

GENERAL CONCLUSIONS

In light of the ''back to basics'' movement and louder and louder calls for ''accountability,'' it is imperative that creative dramatics advocates do more than proclaim a wide variety of beneficial outcomes. The research described above provides a wobbly foundation for further work. As noted in the introduction, creative dramatics research contains far too few concrete descriptions of actual procedures. Too many researchers substitute zeal for rigorous analysis; too many set unreasonable expectations and suffer the disappointment of ''no significant differences.'' Still there is a beginning. Wobbly as it may be, there is a foundation of support for the positive impact of creative dramatics activities in the English classroom on language development, on oral and written fluency, on critical thinking, on literature comprehension, on attitudes toward English and Language Arts, and on the appreciation of literature. Related studies are available which show that creative dramatics experiences can also contribute positively to the development of role-taking skills (Wright, 1972; Lunz, 1974), to the enhancement of self-concept and self-confidence (Irwin, Levy and Shapiro, 1972; Faires, 1976; Bellman, 1974), and to group social skills (Gilmore, 1973).

Our examination of the research also has led us to identify what seem to be certain operational principles. Clearly, for example, implementation of creative dramatics activities is not a fruitful short term proposition.

One-shot experiences and even one week or two week long "units" are simply too brief to yield any kind of significant finding. This seems to be especially true with older children (middle school age or above) where very few of the studies which had treatment periods of less than six or seven weeks resulted in appreciable change in student achievement or attitude.

Finally, our review has shown us how important it is for the classroom teacher to have training and experience in a variety of creative dramatics areas. It is our impression that many of the teachers involved in the studies discussed in this review had little or no training. Too often, the teacher/researchers seemed to have adopted a "laissez-faire" role, setting up the activity and letting the students go. Children engaged in dramatic activities, no less than the most experienced actors on stage, require direction. Without it, their work inevitably lacks order and purpose and they quickly become frustrated or bored or both. The teacher, no less than the able director, must guide dramatic efforts with skill and confidence.

REFERENCES

Bellman, Wanda. "The Effects of Creative Dramatics Activities on Personality As Shown in Student Self-Concept." *Dissertation Abstracts International,* 1974, #35, p. 5668A.

Brandes, P.D. *The Effects of Role Playing by the Culturally Disadvantaged on Attitudes Toward Bidialectalism.* ED 060001, North Carolina University, 1971.

Cercone, Karen L. "The Relative Effects of the Regular Use of Context-Related and Independent Dramatic Activities on Selected Component Skills of Critical Thinking, On Student Attitudes and On the Quality of Dramatic Performances in the English Classroom." Unpublished Ph.D. dissertation, University of Pittsburgh, 1976.

Faires, T. M. "The Effect of Creative Dramatics on Language Development and Treatment Progress of Children in a Psychotherapeutic Nursery." *Dissertation Abstracts International,* 1976, #37, p. 1958A.

Fitzsimmons, Jennifer. "The Play's the Thing: The Use of Creative Dramatics to Teach Vocabulary." Master's Research Paper, University of Pittsburgh, 1975.

Gilmore, S. "Group Processes in Educational Drama: Report of a Pilot Study." *Educational Review,* Vol. 5, #2, Feb., 1973.

Hendrickson, R. H. and Gallegos, F. S. *Using Creative Dramatics to Improve the English Language Skills of Mexican-American Students. Final Report.* California State College, 1972.

Ingersoll, R. L. and Kase, J. B. *Effects of Creative Dramatics on Learning and Retention of Classroom Material.* ED 060000, New Hampshire University, 1971.

Irwin, E., Levy, P. and Shapiro, M. "Assessment of Drama Therapy in a Child Guidance Setting." *Group Therapy and Psychodrama,* Vol. 25, #3, 1972.

Knudson, Richard L. "The Effect of Pupil-Prepared Videotaped Dramas Upon Language Development of Selected Rural Children." *Research in the Teaching of English,* Vol. 5, #1, Spring, 1971.

Lowke, Karil. "The Effects of Using Creative Dramatics as a Technique for Teaching a Narrative Poem." Master's Research Paper, University of Pittsburgh, 1975.

Lunz, Mary Elizabeth. "The Effects of Overt Dramatic Enactment on Communication Effectiveness and Role-Taking Ability." *Dissertation Abstracts International,* 1974, #35, p. 6842A.

Macaluso, Rosemary. "An Experimental Study to Measure the Effects of Two Different Methods of Instruction on the Comprehension and Recall of a Dramatic Work." Master's Research Paper, University of Pittsburgh, 1973.

McCaffrey, M. A. "The Development and Evaluation of an Oral-Dramatic Approach for the Teaching of Poetry in Senior High School." *Dissertation Abstracts International,* 1973, #34, p. 1774A.

Rice, P. C. "Development, Implementation and Evaluation of a 'Moving into Drama' Program to Develop Basic Learning Skills and Language." *Dissertation Abstracts International,* 1972, #32, p. 4929A.

Ridel, Shelby. "An Investigation of the Effects of Creative Dramatics on Ninth Grade Students." Unpublished Ph.D. dissertation, Florida State University, 1975.

Rockefeller, David, Jr., et al. *Coming to Our Senses: The Significance of the Arts for American Education.* Report of The Arts, Education and Americans Panel. McGraw-Hill Book Company, 1977.

Ruttle, Mary Lou. "An Experimental Study of Attitudes of Selected Seventh Grade Students Toward Taking Language Arts As Affected By Participation in Dramatic Activities." Master's Research Paper, University of Pittsburgh, 1975.

Salvo, Donald. "An Experimental Study to Measure the Effects of Performance on the Comprehension and Retention of Dramatic Works." Master's Research Paper, University of Pittsburgh, 1972.

Strickland, Dorothy S. "A Program for Linguistically Different, Black Children." *Research in the Teaching of English,* 1973, #7, p. 79–86.

Wright, M. E. S. "The Effects of Creative Drama on Person Perception." Unpublished Ph.D. dissertation, University of Minnesota, 1972.

PART II
Language, Vocabulary Development, and Reading

Introductory Comments

To many children, creative drama is play; to the teacher, however, it may be used as an instrument for instruction as well as entertainment. The articles in this section reflect the ways practitioners have applied drama in the language arts area.

In their article, "Elementary School Creative Dramatics: Coming to Your Senses," Walter Sawyer and Arlene Leff define creative dramatics as "a process in which one communicates to another or others—some message, feeling, or emotion." The authors provide the reader with examples to visualize this definition, and also they explore the various elements and aims of this technique in the language arts area.

Working with young children in creative dramatics has given John Warren Stewig a unique view of dramatization as a distinct approach to teaching language. "Drama: Integral Part of the Language Arts" not only provides a rationale for its inclusion in the curriculum, but also cites specific examples for its utilization.

Ruth Beaumont Reuse, in "All It Takes is a Little Incentive," writes of her surprise at her students' ability to develop skits based on specific vocabulary words. She provides the reader with examples of how her students came alive during the process.

As one would expect, the teacher has an essential role in providing an environment, both social and physical, in which children can enjoy creative dramatics. Judith Schickedanz describes numerous play themes suitable for preschoolers and lists the necessary props in her article " 'You Be the Doctor and I'll Be Sick': Preschoolers Learn the Language Arts through Play."

Focusing on the contributions of dramatization in the development of children's reading skills, Elinor P. Ross and Betty D. Roe explore, in "Creative Drama Builds Proficiency in Reading," 4 major areas of language arts: listening, reading, writing, and speaking. Ross and Roe also show a variety of ways in which creative dramatics can serve to teach topics such as descriptive words, synonyms, antonyms, and sequence while also serving as a method for diagnosis and remediation.

Specifically relating to vocabulary development, Frederick A. and Barbara Blakely Duffelmeyer describe dramatization as a means for systematically providing a relationship between word meaning and experience. "Developing Vocabulary through Dramatization" shows that "Dramatization helps clarify the meanings of words by indicating experiences associated with them." Thus, it becomes an effective medium which is an improvement over verbal explanations alone.

Andrea Wertheimer began using dramatization in a reading center to motivate reluctant readers and to help her students develop a greater sensitivity toward their classmates. In "Story Dramatization in the Reading Center," Wertheimer's practical advice includes suggestions for materials and procedures, while also describing her problems. Also replete with actual activities is Rose M. Feinberg's "Acting Out Language Skills." The author presents 24 examples of pantomime and written and oral exercises which are ready to be incorporated into a classroom situation.

Elementary School Creative Dramatics: Coming to Your Senses

by Walter Sawyer and Arlene Leff

Of all the nations in the Western world, the United States may have the unhappy distinction of doing the least in children's theater. It is true that thousands of school sponsored productions, almost always imitative of Broadway, are presented across the country each year. However, these spectacles tend to have an elitist nature; the best students tend to get the best parts, and the least talented students don't participate. On the elementary level, parents and grandparents fill classrooms once or twice a year to watch children perform plays in which every child says at least one line. There is certainly a great deal of energy and effort expended on these activities, but one wonders to what purpose. As a public relations device, they seem to do an acceptable job; as a language arts or children's theater activity, they fall short.

EDUCATIONAL PRIORITIES

Deep beneath the surface problem is the fact that children's theater, in our country, is a shoestring operation. England, Sweden, and Germany all have sophisticated programs of children's theater. It is in Russia, however, that children's theater is most highly organized and supported. If there is a privileged class in Russia, it is the children. That point is highly evident in their children's theater. The government commissions the writing of most children's plays, and it is common practice for writers of children's plays to be more highly compensated than writers of plays for adults. The season is ten months long; children are given free tickets and are expected to attend. Although there is often a lack of good scripts, and one may not agree with the amount of state control, the point is that children's theater is solidly supported by the society.

Schumann (1969) described the problem in our country while discussing a study which found that teachers and curriculum advisors felt that a children's theater program might be highly desirable, but not critical to the development of the learner. The educators were most concerned that the new program would take time away from the basic education courses. This clearly contradicts any assumption that the arts are commonly believed to be a fundamental part of American public education. Given our inattention to grooming appreciative audiences, should we even wonder that the country is a nation of television viewers rather than theatergoers?

CREATIVE DRAMATICS

With the current back to basics trend, the future holds little promise as far as increased financial support for children's theater. What course is open to the teacher? The answer, of course, is a program of creative dramatics. This should not be seen as a goal or an objective of education; rather, it is a tool which a teacher can utilize to achieve a number of related language arts objectives, as well as objectives in the affective areas.

Creative dramatics is a process in which one communicates—to another or others—some message, feeling, or emotion. It requires an environment free of grades and criticism. It is not adult directed, but comes from the child. It diverges sharply from the previously described procedure of putting on a play, which was usually written by and for adults, for an audience. The latter is imitative rather than creative.

The most basic element of creative dramatics is the pantomime. This usually looks easy when one sees it done on stage, but actually requires considerable discipline. With children, the focus should be on developing a sense of size, weight, shape, position, and texture. When one asks a child to mime the opening of a door the child will reach up and open a door that would be twelve feet tall if it were real. When asked to move something, it will be done with the hands held parallel to each other as if the thing had no weight or shape. The instruction teaches children not only to communicate by their actions, but by their reactions as well. For example, a basketball is carried differently than a blacksmith's anvil. The pantomime is not a game; it has a deep concentration about it.

Improvisation is more sophisticated than pantomime in that it uses voice. This enables the teacher to use a wide range of possibilities for communicating a message to others. To utilize improvisation, the teacher sets up a situation in which the child can react. One can move from character improvisation, to improvisation of an inanimate object, to the improvisation of a thought or feeling. The situation can begin with a single actor and progress to situations which use two or more actors. The situations should be familiar ones to begin with (e.g., getting an injection at the doctor's) and proceed to the unfamiliar (e.g., expressing the character of a man whose wife just had a baby).

McCaslin (1968) has noted that improvisation is difficult at first, even when there is an understanding of the story and a thorough familiarity with pantomime. Some children will be comfortable with the process while others will not. The latter group will usually express this in a couple of different ways: by refusal or reluctance to take part or by clowning or joking about the task. Both kinds of behavior are seen as a nervousness or inhibition about performing before one's peers. The instruction focuses on the child's concentration of combining body movement and voice to communicate the situation.

Up to this point, only the listening and speaking language modes have been utilized in the creative dramatics process. When a certain mastery of these has been accomplished, the reading and writing modes may be introduced. One way of doing this is to have children read or write a paragraph or story which explains how to do something. The selection is then performed in pantomime or improvisation. One will immediately notice children driving cars without getting in first and building shelves without measuring or cutting the wood. The instruction will focus on such things as following a sequence, clarity of writing, and the translation of the written word into speech and motion.

THE REAL BASICS

From improvisation, there are several possible directions in which the group may proceed. Some examples are miming and music, utilizing masks, exploring the stage, handling scripts, working with lines and cues, props, scenery, costumes, imagination, and character development (Lewis, 1969). Each of these aspects provides a new dimension to creative dramatics. It is important to have both classmates and others observe the polished products of the various activities. Since the focus of creative dramatics is on such things as the individual, self-expression, communication, and discipline, it should be emphasized that those who are watching are observers rather than an audience.

There will always be the temptation (and there is no reason why it should not be succumbed to occasionally) to put all of the aspects of creative dramatics together into a play. It should be noted, however, that a play is a product, and creative dramatics is a process. The aim of the creative dramatics process is not necessarily the production of a play. There are many other legitimate aims of the process, as follows: increasing sensitivity to the thoughts and feelings of others, building a knowledgeable audience, providing positive self-concepts, decreasing shyness/increasing confidence, increasing concentration, providing new relationships with an adult, improving speech and breathing, correlating the language areas, and building an appreciation of process in the arts.

The ultimate aim of the whole process is, of course, to provide one of the many important parts of an education. The arts are not a frill. They are basic. They are laden with the joys, emotions, and sorrows which make up the human experience. Schumann (1969) rightly contends that a person who is callous, indifferent, and impotent in his abilities to hear when he listens and to see when he looks, is just as deficient in his human potentialities as he would be if he could not read or write.

REFERENCES

Lewis, Mary K. *Acting for Children*. New York: John Day, 1969.

McCaslin, Nellie. *Creative Dramatics in the Classroom*. New York: David McKay, 1968.

Schumann, William. The performing arts and the curriculum. *School Music News,* 1969, 32, 32–33, 44–48.

Drama: Integral Part of the Language Arts

by John Warren Stewig

Increasing interest in the values of drama and techniques for doing it contrasts strangely with increased emphasis on accountability and measuring concrete results of teaching cognitive skills. How do teachers interested in drama justify including it in an already crowded program of required subjects? Viewing drama as an integral part of the language arts and a means of teaching about language provides a rationale for including it in the curriculum. Drama as an avenue to more effective teaching of language thus becomes a basic element in the elementary school.

DRAMA AND THE READING PROGRAM

It is logical to begin discussing drama related to reading because many teachers experiment with simple story dramatization in reading classes. True, story dramatization is only one facet of dramatics, but it is easy for teachers who have never tried drama. Creative drama adds vitality and interest to reading programs, no matter which teaching method is used. Whether an old folk tale in a basal reader, a tradebook in an individualized program, or a story made up in a language experience approach, most stories can be dramatized.

In dramatizing, it is important to make a distinction between two ideas and terms which describe them—*interpretation* and *improvisation*. In story dramatization, one begins with interpretation. In this process, the teacher encourages children to choose characters and portray or act out their role. In interpretation, emphasis is on fidelity to the author's story line and on retaining the basic characterization and ideas presented.

In improvisation the basic story is a departure point; children are encouraged to extend, expand, or go beyond the basic thematic material.

They may extend plot forward or backward in time, or expand the story, perhaps by adding a character or enlarging the role played by one in the story. Consider the selfish sisters in Cinderella, for example. You probably never thought much about them, yet new insights might be gained as a result of considering such specific questions as:

1. What things might have made them the way they were?
2. Had they always acted that way? If not, when and why did they change?
3. Were they interested in anything beyond their finery? Did they have any talents, or any friends?

There are other general questions teachers use to encourage children to probe characters in an effort to bring them to life. The character's physical, social and psychological facets need to be considered. *Physical aspects* can be explored through such questions as:

1. What age do we think the character might be? What evidence do we have?
2. What is the appearance, size, and shape of the character? Obviously Mr. Toad would move very differently than would Puss in ''Puss in Boots.''

Related to *social aspects* of the character, we help children think about:

1. What kind of home life do you think the character has? How does he relate to others at home? Stories by Enright and Lenski are particularly effective for exploring family relationships.
2. What kind of relationships does the character have outside of the family? What do these relationships suggest about the character?

Related to *psychological aspects,* we encourage children to consider:

1. What do we know, or can we infer, about the character's feelings? Can we see shifts in feelings? How are these manifested in behaviors?
2. What do the character's actions and words tell us about his attitudes? Do we see changes in these?

Judiciously using questions about any story, you can lead children from *interpretation* to *improvisation,* by asking open-ended questions that encourage thought and action, thus:

1. *Little Red Riding Hood*
   a. What might have happened if the man hadn't come to kill the wolf at the end?
   b. What could have happened if Grandma had realized the wolf was at the door, and she hadn't let him in?

2. *Snow White and the Seven Dwarfs*
    a. How could the queen have found out about Snow White if she had no magic mirror?
    b. Who might have taken Snow White in, if the dwarfs had not?
3. *Jack and the Beanstalk*
    a. What if a beautiful princess had lived at the top of the beanstalk?
    b. What could Jack have done if the beanstalk had wilted when he reached the top?

DRAMA AND THE LITERATURE PROGRAM

Though drama leaders never limit themselves to literature, knowing that movement and sensory experiences are also crucial, using poetry and prose for drama ensures exposure to more literature than children ordinarily encounter in reading programs. Much that the teacher reads to children as part of the literature program can provide departure points for drama.

Probably all teachers would like to provide children with an exposure to poetry as diversified and challenging as possible. One way to do this is to use poetry in drama sessions. As we read widely, we find many poems of use. The most important quality is *action*. As you read, search for verbs appropriate to acting. We find children can:

> wiggle, in the poem "Only My Opinion" by Shannon,
> glibly slither, in the poem "The Spangled Pandemonium" by Brown,
> trudge, in the poem "The Story of Johnny Head-in-Air" by Hoffman, and
> creep, in the poem "A Goblinade" by Jaques.[1]

We also broaden children's acquaintance with prose by using stories as motivation for improvisation. Try using the story of winsome Princess Lenore,[2] or in contrast use episodes from the life of that delightful terror, Harriet.[3] Older boys find endless possibilities in Milo's adventures,[4] while younger boys enjoy the adventures of Peter.[5]

In these, as in any stories for drama, action is crucial. Descriptive passages need to be eliminated, to pare the story to a basic skeleton of action which can be played. The stories need, of course, to be shared completely, before or after their use in drama. This oral reading during the literature period allows children to savor descriptive passages lost during the active involvement of improvising.

ORAL LANGUAGE DEVELOPMENT

Drama encourages several facets of oral facility; the first is *spontaneous oral composition*. Frequently we challenge children to create dialogue, think orally on their feet, compose as they go, in drama sessions. Try giving situation clues, specifying *who, where,* and *what* the problem is. For instance, the teacher might divide children into groups and specify:

> "You've stayed outside playing too late after school. Coming into the kitchen, you see your mother is very angry. Your little brother, who is also there, thinks it's funny. What happens now?"

Children create dialogue and action resulting from the situation. After working on these, the groups present the spontaneous scenes for the other children. In such situations, children create oral dialogue which is not written down and project themselves into the person they are being as they interact verbally.

Related to oral proficiency is conscious understanding of such *paralinguistic elements* as pitch, stress and juncture. Sometimes we show children a picture of a person and ask them to create a voice for the person. At other times we ask children to take a sentence from their improvisation and manipulate it in as many subtle ways as possible. Sentences from the children's dialogue lend themselves to multiple interpretation, and children can try different paralanguage to change the meaning. Such a simple sentence as, "No, I'm not ready to go yet," can change meaning through the use of pitch, stress and juncture.

Children can also understand variety in dialects when we use stories containing dialects as departure points in drama. Using such stories as *Strawberry Girl,*[6] *Thee, Hannah,*[7] and *Roosevelt Grady,*[8] builds an understanding of, and a tolerance for people whose speech patterns are unlike our own. Though we never insist children use dialects while dramatizing, if this happens we encourage it as additional language learning. One author comments:

> "Did the characters speak as they would have in the situation? Amazingly, children are more aware of speech patterns that indicate class and locale than we imagine, and the search for better words to incorporate into the dialogue sends them to the story itself; vocabulary . . . (becomes a) concomitant gain."[9]

Such experiences provide challenges to children's inventiveness, and the results give valuable insights into the expressive qualities of their voices.

NON-VERBAL ELEMENTS

Drama allows us to discover elements of communication too frequently ignored, as children become aware of kinesics and bodily movement. Kinesics, which account for about 55% of the total communicated message, include:

> . . . all bodily gestures, nudges, nods . . . shrugs, and facial gestures such as winks, smiles, sneers and leers—the whole gamut of expressive actions, so important . . . in the small events of daily life.[10]

Too often these elements remain unconscious; we use them, but not by design or purpose. We do sense such obvious discrepancies as when the words say, "Thank you," and the accompanying kinesics say anything but! Children understand that such discrepancies exist. Recently I heard two small children discussing their teacher. One, enamoured by this paragon, said: "Doesn't Miss Brown say the nicest things to us?" The more perceptive child replied: "Yes, but did you ever see how her neck looks when she says them?" Children do have basic awareness of such communication elements and can be made more conscious of them. Unfortunately, we seldom go to the next step to conscious manipulation of kinesics to intensify or augment the words we use.

We challenge children to do this when we ask them to show us how characters might use kinesics in a particular situation. Children delight in planning kinesics for:

> Alice, as the bewildering queen takes her arm,
> the two sisters when the glass slipper slides on Cinderella's foot,
> the wolf as he tries to talk his way into grandmother's house, or
> the wicked queen as she offers the apple to Snow White.

A difference exists between kinesics and *bodily movement;* the latter is larger movement taking place in the context of the available space. Of recent interest because of a popular book,[11] this aspect of communication has long been a concern in drama. As movement education gains momentum, teachers can find materials of help in making children aware of movement as part of drama.[12]

An aspect of body movement interesting to children is animal movement. "The Sandhill Crane" is an especially good poem to use because of the variety of verbs for acting it includes.[13] In it, the crane solemnly *stalks*, the frogs *jump*, the minnows *scuttle*, the chipmunks *stop*, the gophers *hide*, and the mice *whisper*. We talk about the verbs and encourage children to interpret them. Next, children suggest other animals which might be included by the line which mentions "field folk" and we add a variety of animals and movements until we have created an entire menagerie.

We also work to interpret body movement in humans. The problem here is to have children create without resorting to stereotypes. In two exciting new films, a renowned British drama leader works to help children individualize human movement free from stereotypes.[14] To encourage children to consider ways body movement differs among people, we might use a story which provides some large contrasts, for instance between the inquisitive young children and middle-aged Miss Price.[15] This story also provides small contrasts more difficult to achieve in the differences in body movements of the children who are all about the same age. Successful characterization of ebullient Paul, helpful Cary, and bossy Charles entails differences in physical movements.

VOCABULARY DEVELOPMENT

Drama experiences also help develop vocabulary, two types of which are fostered. The first is vocabulary *intrinsic to the art of drama*. The teacher uses drama terms as they are appropriate in discussion, not to consciously teach terms academically, but rather because such terms are more effective than less specialized vocabulary. Thus children might meet such terms as *sincerity,* meaning an honest and consistent response to the motivation, which other leaders refer to as "staying in character." The opposite term is "break," used when a child loses concentration and steps out of character. Leaders regularly use the terms environment, symbol and conflict; children themselves talk about plot, climax and characterization.

There is also vocabulary *intrinsic to the motivation* used, whether prose or poetry. When we use "The Sandhill Crane,"[16] children hear the words *weir* and *tules*. It is important to talk about their meanings to establish the environment of the poem. The teacher does this, not to teach vocabulary consciously, but rather because these two natural elements control such aspects of the improvisation as how children will move, and the kinds of action possible. One moves differently in this environment, among the tules and the weir, than on a dry city street. Plot development possible in this environment would not be possible elsewhere.

These are a few examples of words children may encounter in drama, though words are not taught in a structured way in drama sessions. Rather we share materials containing the words, discussing them informally, using them to pique children's interest and broaden their exposure to words.

DEVELOPMENT OF LISTENING SKILLS

There are two different types of listening skills which drama encourages. The first of these is *basic listening,* defined as listening required for the action of the session to continue. Children must attend to what is going on, in order to say or do whatever comes next. Such listening is necessary in any drama activity, whether the child is responding rhythmically to music or is interpreting a folk tale. This is simple listening for cues, a part of drama whether one is considering first graders working out the adventures of the Gruff family, or sixth graders working out the sequence in *Pandora's Box.* The cues may be to action or words, but children must be actively engaged in listening for the session to continue.

The second type is *evaluative listening,* in which children listen to the verbal interaction to evaluate its effectiveness, and their own ideas about how they might do the same dialogue differently. Frequently the teacher divides the group to allow each child to participate. For example, in *Tom Tit Tot* we have only four characters.[17] To involve every child the teacher may divide the class into groups and each group works on their version of the story. After practice, children share their version with the class. The teacher sets the stage for evaluative listening by discussing the need to listen, pointing out special things to listen for, and reminding children they will have a chance to discuss what they heard when the playing is over. After playing, the group discusses such questions as:

> "What was particularly effective about the voice of the little black thing? How could you tell when it felt different ways? How did the voice change then?
> How could you use your voice to make the little black thing sound different than the way it was done this time?"

Children are then encouraged to work out variations, to experiment using their voices in different ways as they develop their skill of evaluative listening.

DRAMA AND CREATIVE WRITING

Creative drama can both *lead to* and *come from* creative writing. In either case both writing and dramatizing benefit. A leader may motivate children to improvise on an idea or story. As part of the motivation, the teacher explains that at the close of the experience, the children will write down what has happened. With young children this may be simple recording of plot: with older children it may include more sophisticated descriptions of such ephemeral elements as paralanguage and kinesics. After children write, a profitable discussion can ensue about differences between what individual children wrote, and discrepancies among observers' reports of an event. It is also logical to discuss what is easy to describe in writing, and the more elusive aspects to write down. Such discussions lead logically, especially with older children, to considerations of differences between the written form of a play and its physical manifestation when brought to life by actors. The goal of drama is not formal play-making; such discussions nonetheless give children insights into theatre, and stimulate them to ask questions about aspects of formal drama not ordinarily considered in school.

Drama can also *come from* creative writing. The teacher may motivate children to write. Then, some of their stories can be used as bases for improvisation. Invariably children will want to know why their story was not chosen, and this can lead to a discussion of characteristics of good motivations for drama. Stories effective for playing usually include:

> clearly defined, active characters with which children can identify,
> a logical form with an arresting beginning,
> a clear and uncluttered story line, leading to
> a climax and satisfying conclusion.

Often examination and discussion of stories leads to the request, "May I rewrite mine so we can use it?" Rewrite sessions which follow, as the teacher helps children edit and strengthen characterization, plot, conflict, and dialogue, can be helpful not only in producing more story motivations for drama, but also in helping children write stories of more intrinsic value as creative writing.

SUMMARY

Creative drama can be an integral part of an elementary language program, because it serves as an avenue of approach to the other language arts. Teachers interested in drama can convince parents, supervisors and principals of the validity of drama if they emphasize the contribution drama makes to learnings in the reading and literature programs, oral language development, non-verbal communication, vocabulary development, listening skills and creative writing. Teachers know children will grow in other ways—social and emotional growth has been well described elsewhere—but it may be easier to proselytize for drama if teachers emphasize the richness drama adds to the language arts.

NOTES

1. All of these are included in *The Arbuthnot Anthology of Children's Literature,* by May H. Arbuthnot. Glenview: Scott, Foresman and Co., 1971.

2. Thurber, James. *Many Moons*. Harcourt, Brace and Jovanovich, 1943.

3. Fitzhugh, Louise. *Harriet The Spy*. Harper and Row, 1964.

4. Juster, Norton. *The Phantom Tollbooth*. Random House, 1961.

5. Keats, Ezra Jack. *Peter's Chair*. Harper and Row, 1967.

6. Lenski, Lois. *Strawberry Girl*. Lippincott, 1945.

7. DeAngeli, Marguerite. *Thee, Hannah*. Doubleday, 1940.

8. Shotwell, Louisa. *Roosevelt Grady*. Grossett and Dunlap, 1963.

9. Henry, Mable W. *Creative Experiences in Oral Language*. NCTE, 1967.

10. Lefevre, Carl. *Linguistics, English and the Language Arts*. Allyn and Bacon, Inc., 1970, pp. 174–5.

11. Fast, Julius. *Body Language*. M. Evans, 1970.

12. Barlin, Anne and Paul. *The Art of Learning Through Movement*. Ritchie, 1971.

13. Austin, Mary. "The Sandhill Crane," in *Arbuthnot,* op.cit., p. 53.

14. *Dorothy Heathcote Talks to Teachers, Parts One and Two*. From Northwestern University Film Library, Evanston, Ill.

15. Norton, Mary. *The Magic Bed-Knob*. Hyperion Press, 1943.

16. Austin, op.cit.

17. Ness, Evaline. *Tom Tit Tot*. Scribner's, 1965.

All It Takes Is a Little Incentive

by Ruth Beaumont Reuse

The clown of my third period English class made his grand entrance from the hallway "hee-hawing" loudly and kicking up his heels. He was followed by a classmate who snapped a towel and yelled, "Giddap there, Jed! Giddap!"

The class giggled. I sat at the back of the room surprised but delighted at the enthusiasm with which these tenth graders had taken up a spur-of-the-moment assignment. Right in front of my desk the "mule" stopped kicking and refused to move another inch. His "farmer" classmate tried pushing and pulling, but neither worked. He then walked to the blackboard where he wrote the word OBSTINATE in large letters. "That's my mule," he said with a grin. "He's *obstinate,* but I'll handle him."

Then he pulled a candy bar from his pocket and dangled it in front of the "mule" who immediately began moving with loud hee-haws toward the candy. The "farmer" student returned to the blackboard and wrote INCENTIVE. He turned to the class and announced, "Yeah, ol' Jed's *obstinate,* but I can handle him. All he needs is a little *incentive!*"

I had not expected such a fantastic performance a week earlier when I casually made the assignment to work up skits based on vocabulary words. In fact, the only response was a group-stare for which students are famous. Yet they had come through with gratifying originality. The farmer and his mule had definitely impressed the meanings of "obstinate" and "incentive" much more deeply on the minds of the class than any explanation or example I could have provided.

Cathy followed the mule with a totally different but equally clever presentation. She tacked three magazine pictures of "Breck girls" to the bulletin board and announced that she was going to conduct a class poll. "You will be asked to vote for the girl you think is the most *vivacious.*" She wrote the word clearly on the blackboard and went on. "Now remember, class, your decision must be based only on *vivacious* qualities: liveliness of spirit, sparkling eyes, fresh glow, high color—anything that suggests being full of life. Judge each girl on these qualities and nothing else.''

Again the word definition came alive through its use in a realistic and *visual* situation. There were other skits. Some students presented their single word assignment by themselves. Others grouped together to create skits based on several words. I was amazed at their creativity and sat back to enjoy the show. One girl CONJURED up out of the wastebasket a genie with a PROTUBERANT nose; another completely ENSCONCED her best friend in a role of leftover Christmas wrap which she then EMBELLISHED with leftover bows.

During that class period and the next one, the students did skits which clearly demonstrated the basic definitions of thirty-four vocabulary words taken from a reading assignment. It was occasionally necessary for me to point out additional meanings and uses, but the skits served as the basis for remembering the words. Discussion and review on the third day indicated that most students had no trouble identifying the words with their meanings. The skits had provided a meaningful association tool as well as a refreshing approach to word study.

The climax of this assignment came on the second day when David and Chuck, who had begged me to let them be last but would not tell me why, suddenly jumped up when their turn came and began pointing to the corner and yelling that there was a mouse in the room. Since a mouse was a very real possibility in our under-the-stadium classroom, this announce-ment created wild chaos for a few seconds while David and Chuck just stood by and laughed. When things settled down they calmly wrote on the blackboard the words INCITE and PRETEXT. They explained that they had just *incited* the class to riot on the *pretext* that there was a mouse in the room!

"You Be the Doctor and I'll Be Sick": Preschoolers Learn the Language Arts through Play

by Judith Schickedanz

Around the age of two, children begin to show characteristic behavior that is commonly known as "pretending." Those who study young children refer to this behavior as *dramatic* or *symbolic* play. The term, dramatic, refers to the make-believe or reality-suspending quality of the activity; through actions and words children create characters and settings and tell a story (Garvey 1977). The term, symbolic, refers to the representational nature of the play; children use themselves or objects as symbols in order to represent someone or something else. Play is not unlike other symbolic activities, such as talking and drawing, in this regard (Furth 1969).

At first, dramatic or symbolic play is very simple; children reenact their own activities; for example, they may pretend to sleep, eat, or cry. Later, they use inanimate objects such as dolls or stuffed animals to portray everyday activities; they make the doll sleep or cry, or make the dog eat. In time, children pretend that they are someone else, perhaps a mother or father, a teacher, a firefighter, or a doctor. When dramatic play reaches this role-taking stage, it becomes highly social, and children actively use language to structure and sustain it (Hunt 1961; Garvey 1977; Smilansky 1971). In fact, in studies of language production in preschool classrooms, children have been found to be more verbal in the dramatic play situation than in any other (Marshall 1961). This finding is not surprising when one considers the vital functions that language plays in dramatic play. According to Garvey (1977, p. 86), "In order to pretend with a companion, the child needs techniques for indicating who he is, what he is doing, what objects represent (or what objects have been invented), and where he is (at home, at work, on a train)."

An example of how children use language to establish features of their play is also provided by Garvey (1977, p. 87):

Component		**Example**
Role:	self	I'm a working lady at work.
	partner	Are you going to be a bride?
	both	We can both be wives.
Plan:	self	I gotta drive to the shopping center.
	partner	Pretend you hated baby fish.
	both	We have to eat. Our dinner's ready.
Object:	change	This is a train. (putting suitcase on the sofa)
	invent	Now this is cheesecake and this is ice cream. (pointing to empty places on a plate)
Settings		Here we are at the doctor's office.
		This is our house.

Traditionally, probably because of the influence of Freud, the value of dramatic play has been thought to be mostly socio-emotional or therapeutic. Only recently, largely due to the work of Piaget (1961), has play's contribution to cognitive and language development been seriously considered. It is for this reason that even though preschool and kindergarten teachers have for years included "house play" in their programs, they have not always recognized its contributions to the child's learning, and they have not always actively supported its full development. This article will present ideas for creating play environments in which children can have experiences with all of the language arts.

PROVIDING PROPS FOR PLAY

Even though young children are known for their ingenuity in using just about anything at hand as playthings, teachers can facilitate children's dramatic play by providing objects that have been thoughtfully selected for this purpose. Over the course of the school year, different collections of props can be provided to develop various play themes. Props that would be good ones to support a number of play themes are listed in Table 1.

THE TEACHER'S ROLE

The physical environment, created through the use of space and props, is essential for supporting play, but it is not enough; the teacher must lend other kinds of support as well.

Providing Background Experiences

Children adopt roles and imitate behaviors that they have been able to observe. Play in the classroom can be enhanced by providing experiences that will familiarize children with various settings and roles.

Trips are ideal for helping children acquire this kind of knowledge. Children can see firsthand how similar foods are stored together in a grocery store, how signs are used to label the various food departments, how customers use shopping lists, what stock persons, butchers, and cashiers do, and how people in a grocery store relate to one another. The teacher's questions can guide children's observations: "How are all the foods on this shelf alike?" "How could we find the foods we want without having to search throughout the entire store?" "How does the cashier know which keys of the cash register to punch?" "Why do you think that daddy is yelling at that little girl?"

When a trip is not feasible, background experiences can be provided in other ways. Often, teachers can draw upon children's own everyday experiences. Through discussions, children can be helped to reflect about trips to the grocery store that they may have made with their parents. In addition, teachers can ask children to make observations on future trips: "Watch the cashiers to see if you can figure out how they know which keys to punch." "See if you can find out what other foods are stored near the milk." A newsletter to parents containing an explanation of the plans for setting up a classroom grocery store, and a few suggestions for ways that they can help their children make observations could lend additional support to children's learning. Later, when children are asked to bring a food or household product container to school to be used as a prop in the play store, parents will understand its purpose.

Books, films, and pictures can also be used to provide background experiences. These resources work especially well when children can discuss the ideas expressed, and can relate them to their own, firsthand experiences.

Becoming a Partner in Play

Often, when the play area is in use, the teacher can join in. Sometimes, children will invite the teacher to take a role: "You be the doctor and I'll be sick." These invitations lead to excellent opportunities for introducing new ideas and language that can serve to extend children's play: "Tell me about your symptoms." "How long have you been sick?" "Let me listen to your lungs through the stethoscope while you breathe deeply and slowly."

When playing house, a teacher who has assumed the role of parent might prepare a shopping list for use at the grocery store. (If the classroom is large enough to accommodate play areas for both a house and a store, complex interactions between the two areas can occur.) The help of other "family members" can be solicited through questions such as, "What shall we have for dinner?" or "What ingredients will we need if we're going to make a cake and spaghetti?"

Teachers must exercise great care when participating in children's dramatic play. This is not the place for "lessons" and "lectures." The teacher's behavior should be dictated in large part by the children. Teacher-initiated ideas that are not quickly integrated into the play by the children should be forgotten by the teacher. As Garvey (1977, p. 82) has pointed out, "make-believing is not entirely free; one cannot behave *ad libitum*. There are restrictions and, apparently, guidelines for behavior, since a 'wrong' move will often be pointed out by the child." In addition, children often represent actions only schematically, rather than in full. For a child, preparing a shopping list may consist only of obtaining a small, blank piece of paper, or of placing a few scribbles on a piece of paper, or of writing a word or two. The technique of moving into the children's play, introducing a few ideas, and the moving out again, which is used by many teachers, provides for teacher input, but insures that the children can move the play in the direction that they wish.

Helping Children Solve Problems

Dramatic play situations provide an excellent environment for problem solving. What is to be done when all of the food cartons will not fit on the shelves in the play store? What can be used to make play money? What should be done when too many children want to play at the same time in the small play area? And what can be done when two children want to be the mother, and no one wants to be the baby?

With the teacher's help, such problems can be solved, and in the process, children's thinking and language can be extended. The extra food containers might be placed on a shelf in the teacher's closet. This place could become known as "the warehouse," and children could obtain new cartons from here as the ones in constant use in the store wear out. Or, perhaps the extra cartons could be used for art projects. Children may want to sort through all of the cartons to select for art use only those for which they have a duplicate. The teacher would offer suggestions for solutions to such problems, and would ask the children for their suggestions too: "Do you think we could figure out a way for two mothers to play here?" "Could a doll be your baby?" "What do you think we could use to make our money shiny?"

DRAMATIC PLAY AND THE CHILDREN'S LEARNING

Children learn about language in all of its forms in the dramatic play environment, as well as from support activities. Talking is vital to dramatic play, and as has already been noted, children talk more in this than in any other classroom setting. The meaningful context in which talking occurs, and the natural requirements for effective communication, such as when problems arise, are ideal for supporting language development. In addition, play props provide good opportunities for children to learn new words such as *stethoscope, skeleton, x-ray, scale, coupons, spatula, skillet,* and *cash register.*

Dramatic play also provides meaningful opportunities through which children can be introduced to reading and writing. Food cartons are wonderful sources of words. The neighborhoods through which children might travel on a trip to the grocery store are full of words too—on street signs, billboards, and storefronts. A children's "cookbook" and "telephone" book provided for house play invite reading and perhaps writing too, if children are asked to help make them. Similarly, an "appointment" book used in doctor play, and a "logbook" used in firefighter play also invite children to write, even though for many preschoolers the writing will take the form of scribbles.

When paper and pencils are provided as props for play, children often make their own materials, thus creating additional opportunities for reading and writing. In a classroom in which I recently observed, a few children used the paper and pencils in the house-play area to make invitations for a pretend birthday party. For awhile, the actual play, which had involved cake-baking activities, stopped, and the children worked on the invitations, seeking help to spell and form the letters for "Happy Birthday" from a nearby teacher. (Interruptions of play to prepare materials or to solve problems occur frequently.) It is interesting to note here that in her study of early readers, Durkin (1966) discovered many children who became intrigued with paper, pencils, and writing, before learning to read. She dubbed these children "paper and pencil kids." If children were routinely supplied with paper and pencil props in play settings, they might use them as a matter of course just as they use dress-up clothes, dishes, and pots and pans.

Perhaps the most appealing aspect of helping young children learn the language arts through play is that children learn to talk by talking, to write by writing, and to read by reading, which, according to many who study the acquisition of these skills, is the best way to learn them (Macnamara 1976; Smith 1971). But to say that it is the children who must be active in acquiring these skills is not to say that they learn them "all on their own."

As this article has pointed out, the teacher plays a vital role by providing a rich physical and social environment that is essential to support children's play.

REFERENCES

Durkin, D. *Children Who Read Early*. New York: Teachers College Press, 1966.

Furth, H. *Piaget and Knowledge*. Englewood Cliffs, NJ: Prentice-Hall, Inc., 1969.

Garvey, C. *Play*. Cambridge, MA: Harvard University Press, 1977.

Hunt, J. McV. *Intelligence and Experience*. New York: Ronald Press, 1961.

Macnamara, J. "First and Second Language Learning: Same or Different?" *Journal of Education* 158 (1976): pp. 39–54.

Marshall, H. P. "Relations Between Home Experience and Children's Use of Language in Play Interactions with Peers." *Psychological Monographs* 75 (1961): pp. 9–15.

Piaget, J. *Play Dreams and Imitation in Childhood*. New York: W.W. Norton and Company, Inc., 1962.

Smilansky, S. "Can Adults Facilitate Play in Children?: Theoretical and Practical Considerations." In *Play,* edited by N. Curry. Washington, D.C.: National Association for the Education of Young Children, 1971.

Smith F. *Understanding Reading: A Psycholinguistic Analysis of Reading and Learning to Read,* New York: Holt, Rinehart, and Winston, 1971.

Table 1. Dramatic Play Themes and Props

House Play

1. Kitchen furniture: a stove, sink, refrigerator, table and chairs, shelves.
2. Tablecloth or place mats.
3. Small chest of drawers and doll bed.
4. Artificial flowers.
5. Several dolls and stuffed animals.
6. Dolls' clothes, blankets, and bottles.

Table 1. Dramatic Play Themes and Props (continued)

7. Old adult clothes: hats, gloves, jackets, neckties, scarves, jewelry.
8. Plastic replicas of fruits and vegetables.
9. An assortment of dishes, silverware, pots and pans, and cooking utensils.
10. Empty containers from food, cleaning products, and toiletry items.
11. Dustpan and small broom.
12. Play telephones.
13. Brown paper bags or plastic net bags to use for "shopping" or "picnicking" trips.
14. Container of play-dough.
15. A "cookbook" consisting of a collection of recipe charts used in classroom cooking projects.
16. A "telephone book" consisting of children's names, street addresses, and telephone numbers.
17. Paper, pencils, and envelopes.
18. Wall plaques with appropriate sayings such as "Home Sweet Home."

Fire Station Play

1. Climbing box or building blocks to use in creating a fire station.
2. Firefighter hats.
3. Old shirts to use as firefighters' jackets.
4. Small lengths of garden hose to use as water hoses.
5. A bell to use as a fire alarm.
6. Old flashlights.
7. Play telephones.
8. A sign that says FIRE STATION.
9. Very simple labelled maps of the classroom for use in locating "fires."
10. Picture posters with appropriate fire safety messages.
11. A large "log" book made with blank sheets of paper.
12. Pencils.

Doctor's Office Play

1. Old, white skirts and blouses for use as doctor and nurse dress-up clothes.
2. Medical props such as stethoscopes, popsicle sticks or straws (thermometer), strips of white cloth (bandages), plastic syringes, cotton balls, and old flashlights.
3. Play telephones.

Table 1. Dramatic Play Themes and Props (continued)

4. Dolls and dolls' clothes.
5. DOCTOR IS IN and DOCTOR IS OUT signs.
6. An "appointment" book for the receptionist.
7. Pencils.
8. Model of clock face with hands that move.
9. An alphabet letter or picture "eye chart."
10. Exposed x-ray films obtained from a doctor.
11. Poster showing the human skeleton, or body parts.

Grocery Store Play

1. A shelving unit.
2. Cardboard boxes that can serve as cases for "dairy products" or "produce." (Place smaller box inside larger one to make a raised surface.)
3. A large variety of empty containers from foods and other household products.
4. Plastic fruits and vegetables.
5. Play money.
6. A cash register (toy or old real one).
7. Large food sale poster obtained from local grocers.
8. Brown paper bags of various sizes.
9. Newspaper pages containing food ads.
10. OPEN and CLOSED signs.
11. Old shirts for store employee costumes.
12. A kitchen scale to weigh produce.
13. A large selection of food and household products coupons clipped from magazines and the newspaper.
14. A small pad or small pieces of paper, and pencils.
15. Magnetic board and letters to use in making signs for special sales.

Creative Drama Builds Proficiency in Reading

by Elinor P. Ross and Betty D. Roe

Creative drama includes all forms of improvised drama, such as dramatic play, pantomime, puppet shows, and story dramatization. It is created spontaneously by the players themselves as an expression of their feelings or an interpretation of the characters in a story. Only in recent years have educators recognized its value for enhancing a child's learning experiences.

Creative drama can be an effective way to develop a child's reading proficiency. It is not meant to replace reading instruction, but it can be used as a supplementary tool for motivating children to read and for reinforcing reading skills in a way that makes reading fun. Creative drama can also be used as an alternate approach to reading instruction when traditional methods fail.

All four of the major language arts—listening, speaking, reading, and writing—are involved in creative drama. It motivates children to listen and speak, and encourages them to read and write as they research background material for use in dramatizations.

In order to learn to read with ease, a child needs certain skills that may be developed through creative drama.

Directionality and visual perception can be developed. For example, the teacher can be a toymaker who has turned children into dolls that can only move to the left or right as directed. In another game, the teacher stands with her back to the class and the children become her shadows by imitating her movements as she calls, ''Raise your right leg,'' or ''Wave your left hand.''

Children can become more skillful in visual discrimination by using their bodies to form shapes. Either with partners or alone, they can copy numerals and letter shapes with their bodies in order to learn them kinesthetically.

Tucker (1971) suggested developing discrimination by using a sound effects record as a stimulus for guessing different sounds. The children respond by making the sounds with their voices or depicting the sounds with their bodies. Siks (1958, p. 280) felt that children would improve in auditory discrimination by

> becoming a train engine that moves fast or slow; a train with a light load or a heavy one; a train that has a big or a little engine; a train that whistles with a loud or soft whistle; a train that is near or far away; a train that is a "diesel, electric, or heavy freight."

Children who know they will be dramatizing a story after they hear it will have a good reason for listening carefully to the sequence, dialogue, main ideas, and details of the story. They must pay careful attention in order to recreate the story and to interpret the characters as they appeared. They also must listen respectfully to each other in order to communicate sensibly during their improvisation.

Oral expression develops naturally and easily in the informal atmosphere provided by creative drama. Children learn to speak spontaneously and fluently because they need to keep the story going. Many of them lose their self-consciousness when they become characters in stories. Smilansky's (1968) study of kindergarten children revealed that increased participation in dramatic play resulted in more verbalization.

Shaw (1968, p. 199) claimed that creative drama

> should help children to become aware of the ways in which words, inflections, and gesture shape and convey meaning; it should give them an opportunity to develop their skills in encoding and decoding communications.

Children who are communicating a dramatic situation to an audience discover the importance of choosing the right words, of speaking expressively, and of enunciating clearly.

Quite often creative drama can provide the motivation for improving articulation. Hayes (1970) reported that school children who spoke "pidgin" English developed better intonation and clearer enunciation as a result of participating in a creative drama program. In their studies, Ludwig (1963) and Woolf and Myers (1968) showed that creative drama produced greater improvement in articulation than other methods of instruction.

Perryman (1962) pointed out that children begin to understand the need for reading written symbols when engaged in dramatic play. The youngster who plays truck driver reads road signs and a child who shops in a grocery store must be able to recognize labels on cans.

BUILDING READING SKILLS

Reading skills are developed through creative drama in a variety of ways. Children recognize the need for increasing their vocabularies because they have a real purpose for knowing the right words while they are in character. By acting out such descriptive words as *wicked, starving,* or *greedy* from the stories they read, they are clarifying the meanings of these words. At the same time they may work on expanding their vocabularies by thinking of words which mean the same as the words they are portraying. Children may suggest *bad* and *evil* as synonyms for *wicked*.

Children have fun learning the meanings of antonyms by playing "Opposites." The teacher has word cards containing pairs of antonyms. Two children come to the teacher and each takes one word card from a set of antonyms. They dramatize their words in turn and their classmates guess what the word pair is. When a correct answer is given, the cards are held up by the actors for the class to see, and another pair of children choose words.

Vocabulary can also be developed through "Magic Modifiers," in which the students portray their concepts of a *greedy* giant, a *dejected* giant, and an *angry* giant, as well as the ideas of eating *delicately* and eating *voraciously*. Another game which can help build vocabulary is "Varied Verbs." In it, the children act out verbs which are close in meaning but have slightly different connotations: *walked, sauntered, shuffled, strode,* and others. Children learn how suffixes can change the meanings of words as they pretend to be *sleepy* or *sleeping*. Borden (1970) reported another activity designed to turn action words into sight words. She would write the name of a child on the board along with an action word in this manner: "Jack, jump!" The child named would be expected to perform the action. Borden found this approach to be successful with children who were unable to recognize any other words.

Sentence comprehension can be developed by a game called "The Sentence Says" in which a sentence is read by a child or a group of children, and the readers act out what the sentence says. Paragraph comprehension can be developed by a parallel game called "Play the Paragraph" in which the children read and act out a paragraph.

To develop comprehension of an entire selection, story dramatization can be used. When the children read (or listen to) the story to be dramatized, they must make inferences about the reasons for actions of certain characters, the basic natures of the different characters and their emotions, and incidents which led up to the main events in the story. They need to use critical reading skills to determine whether the story is real or make-believe and whether the characters are believable in the situations in which they are found. Careful attention to the details in the story is necessary or the dramatization will not be accurate, and if sequence is not carefully noted, the play will not progress smoothly and logically. Visualization skills must be used to picture the setting and characters involved in the story.

Visualization is the ability to picture what the written word is describing. One game, "Stretching the Imagination," is especially good for this. In it the students are given a list of things to which they must react. In order to react appropriately, they are asked to visualize the appearance, taste, smell, and feel of the named object or place. Examples of things to be named include sugar cookies, lemons, skunks, lizards, the seashore, and a snowy hillside.

"Who Am I?" is a game that helps develop a special type of visualization—visualization of the characteristics of people in selections being read. Children read a story and then take turns walking, running, and talking in a way that portrays one character from the story. The rest of the group tries to identify the character.

To develop the skill of recognizing sequence, the students can read nursery rhymes and then act out each rhyme in sequence. Good choices include "Little Jack Horner" and "Little Miss Muffett."

Dramatization of certain types of literature can greatly enhance the children's comprehension of the written material. Borden (1970) reported that children who had difficulty understanding the morals of fables which were read to them understood the morals after reliving the fables through dramatization. Dramatization of stories also can help the children to sense the mood of the selections.

After a child has been involved in acting out a number of stories, his oral reading expression will begin to improve, for he will have begun to "think the dialogue" in terms of oral presentation as he reads. He will be more aware of the clues to oral expression embodied in the punctuation if he has been guided to attend to such clues when preparing for a dramatization.

Story dramatization also provides motivation for children to do research on the period in which the story is set or on the characters in the story. Children are thus enticed to use encyclopedias, history books, and biographies to make sure their presentations are authentic.

Creative reading skills can be developed by having the children read a story up to a certain point and then act out the way they think it will end, or by having them change one happening in a story they have read and act out how that would affect the ending. If they can do these things adequately, they are truly able to read "beyond the lines."

Carlton and Moore (1966) compared reading gains of culturally disadvantaged children who participated in self-directive dramatization of stories as a part of their reading instruction and culturally disadvantaged children who received traditional basal reading instruction. They found significantly greater improvement in reading in the group which used self-directive dramatization. They also found a correlation between progress in reading and improvement in self-concept.

Creative drama can be a tremendous motivational force for reading. When students wish to do a dramatization, they may be encouraged to read numerous selections to find one that is just right to use. After a story has been chosen for dramatization, the children will be motivated to read it again in order to visualize the setting and characters adequately, get the sequence firmly in mind, and decide upon the scene divisions. They will also be drawn to other sources to do research on the period or characters.

Once they have been introduced to a type of literature or particular time period or character through creative drama, some of the children will become fascinated with this new experience and will seek to read more along these lines. For example, Hayes (1970) reported that drama has been effective in leading Hawaiian children to the reading of Hawaiian myths and legends.

According to Rike (1973–74), creative drama can serve as a group method of diagnosis and remediation. Some misconceptions of words are revealed while the children are dramatizing a situation. These misconceptions can be corrected as the teacher guides the children toward more accurate concepts. Siks (1958) pointed out that teachers can check reading comprehension by having them act out the answers to questions about the story or encouraging them to become characters from the story. Children show their awareness of story sequence, their knowledge of details, their understanding of the characters and their sensitivity to the mood of the story by the way they play their parts. If weaknesses in any of these areas are revealed, the teacher can plan additional activities.

The numerous examples in this article indicate that creative drama can make an important contribution to the development of children's reading skills. Perhaps the most exciting part of this contribution is the fact that the children are learning while they are enjoying themselves—to them creative drama is play, but it is certainly highly rewarding play!

REFERENCES

Bordan, Sylvia Diane. *Play as Teaching Tools in the Elementary School.* West Nyack, N.Y.: Parker Publishing Co., 1970.

Carlton, Lessie and Robert H. Moore. "The Effects of Self-Directive Dramatization on Reading and Self-Concept of Culturally Disadvantaged Children." *The Reading Teacher,* vol. 20, no. 2 (November 1966), pp. 125–30.

Hayes, Eloise. "Drama, Big News in English." *Elementary English,* vol. 47 (January 1970), pp. 13–16.

Ludwig, Charlotte E. The Effect of Creative-Dramatic Activities upon the Articulation Skills of Kindergarten Children. Unpublished master's thesis, University of Pittsburgh, 1963.

Perryman, Lucille C. "Dramatic Play and Cognitive Development." *The Journal of Nursery Education,* vol. 17 (September 1962), pp. 185–88.

Rike, Elizabeth. "Self-Study Creative Dramatics." *Knox County Title I Report,* 1973–74.

Shaw, Ann Marie. The Development of a Taxonomy of Educational Objectives in Creative Dramatics in the United States Based on Selected Writings in the Field. Unpublished doctoral dissertation. Columbia University, 1968. (Microfilm)

Siks, Geraldine Brain. *Creative Dramatics: An Art for Children.* New York, N.Y.: Harper & Row, 1958.

Smilansky, Sara. *The Effects of Sociodramatic Play on Disadvantaged Pre-school Children.* New York, N.Y.: John Wiley & Sons, 1968.

Tucker, JoAnne Klineman. The Use of Creative Dramatics as an Aid in Developing Reading Readiness with Kindergarten Children. Unpublished doctoral dissertation, University of Wisconsin, 1971.

Woolf, Gerald and Mary Jane Myers. "The Effect of Two Ear Training Procedures on the Improvement of Auditory Discrimination and Articulation." *Exceptional Children,* vol. 34, no. 9 (May 1968), pp. 659–65.

Developing Vocabulary through Dramatization

by Frederick A. Duffelmeyer and Barbara Blakely Duffelmeyer

Most methods of teaching vocabulary fall under the general heading "direct"—characterized by deliberate teaching of word meanings, usually with explicit teacher guidance. In contrast, "incidental" methods are characterized by the absence of deliberate instruction in word meanings, for example, the "wide reading" method.

Although many teachers favor a direct method, they recognize that there may be dangers involved. Dale (1969, p. 33) is among those who have voiced concern: "One of education's hazards lies in the way in which words are learned. Often they are floating items unattached to real experience, and as a result the knowledge is merely verbal. The shell of meaning is there, but the kernel is missing."

One direct method avoids this difficulty: tying the vocabulary to student experiences. McKee (1937, p. 280) considered the use of experiences "the most potent procedure in developing a meaning vocabulary." Tinker (1952) also emphasized the use of rich and varied, firsthand and vicarious experiences for developing students' vocabularies, as did Petty, Herold and Stoll—otherwise, "vocabulary teaching will result in surface verbalization" (Petty, Herold and Stoll 1968, p. 12).

Given that the meaning of words depends on the experiences that stand back of them, it follows that an approach to teaching vocabulary which relies primarily on experience would foster depth of word meaning and subsequently correct interpretation in reading. However, given the constraints of the usual classroom, how can one possibly provide enough experiences to make an "experiential" approach practical?

VICARIOUS EXPERIENCES

It is easy to agree with Frazier (1970) that new words are learned when taught as labels for direct experiences, but word meanings can be developed by means of secondhand experiences as well. Thus, the task is to create maximal vicarious experiences.

Teaching vocabulary through experience has long been used by foreign language teachers (Brooks 1964, Rivers 1968, Sandstrom 1970). The foreign language teacher who simply provides students with a list of words and their equivalents is certainly not deepening the learner's grasp of word meaning. Had each word been introduced in an experiential context, it would have been made more meaningful and more useful to the student.

In the foreign language lesson, as in the reading lesson, new words may be introduced in terms of other words with which the students are already familiar, using simple dialogs or short dramatizations. As Brooks (1964, p. 145) pointed out, "the learner finds a personal interest in what he is saying and a possible use far beyond the classroom for the expressions which he masters. Time is not wasted in learning isolated words and isolated sentences that may be credited with logical meaning but are devoid of psychological meaning. Rightly constructed, all dialogs have a dramatic potential that can be exploited to advantage in the classroom."

Thus, an effective medium for vocabulary instruction is dramatization. Dramatization helps clarify the meanings of words by indicating experiences associated with them. Granted, such secondhand experiences are not as potent as direct ones, but they are certainly an improvement over verbal explanation alone (Harris and Sipay 1971, p. 280).

As an example, consider the following scene, which is designed to clarify the word *celerity*.

Setting: Booth at a carnival. A small crowd is gathered around a carnival worker.

Worker: Step right up! Step right up! Is there any among you who would dare to risk a small amount to prove that the hand is not quicker than the eye? You, sir, you look like a man of action. For the mere sum of 25 cents—just one quarter of a dollar—I will demonstrate such quickness as you have never seen.

Man: (Shrugs) Why not? (Takes a quarter from his pocket and throws it on the counter)

Worker: (Gesturing to three small cups bottom side up on the counter) Witness. Three cups and a tiny object no larger than a pearl. (Holds it up so all can see) Under the middle of the three it goes, and where it stops nobody

	knows! (Maneuvers cups, then stops) Now sir, would you care to point to the cup under which the tiny object lies?
Man:	(Points to one of the cups) This one. (Worker lifts up the cup. The object is not there. The worker has a gleeful look on his face.)
Woman:	(Turns to person standing next to her) Did you see the celerity with which he moved his hands? So swiftly. It was amazing!
Worker:	(Having overheard) Did I hear the word "celerity"? Celerity is *all* in this trade. If I'm not quick, I'm out of busines Crowd beginning to move away) Step right up! Step right up!

Following the enactment of a scene, the teacher can pose questions to reinforce the concept. Appropriate questions for the preceding scene might include "Which character in this scene displayed celerity?" "What other situations can you think of where celerity would be important?"

One other advantage to using dramatizations is that they give opportunity for a discussion of speech levels and the use of words in specific social contexts, such as speech versus writing, or casual conversation versus formal situations. In the preceding example, for instance, whether or not a student remarks that "people don't talk like that," the teacher can initiate a discussion of situations where *celerity* would and would not be likely to be used, and why.

Most approaches to vocabulary development are criticized as being unsystematic (Dale, O'Rourke and Bamman 1971). However, it is far worse that they are inconsistent with what is known about the relationship between word meaning and experience. As Dale (1969, p. 33) said: "a reader must possess some background of experience that can be tied to the words he reads, for otherwise they can mean little indeed." Dramatization is one means of providing such a background.

REFERENCES

Brooks, Nelson. *Language and Language Learning: Theory and Practice.* New York, N.Y.: Harcourt Brace Jovanovich, 1964.

Dale, Edgar. *Audiovisual Methods in Teaching.* New York, N.Y.: Holt, Rinehart and Winston, Inc., 1969.

Dale, Edgar, Joseph O'Rourke and Henry Bamman. *Techniques of Teaching Vocabulary.* Palo Alto, Cal.: Field Educational Publications, Inc., 1971.

Frazier, Alexander. "Developing a Vocabulary of the Senses." *Elementary English,* vol. 47, no. 2 (February 1970), pp. 176–84.

Harris, Albert and Edward Sipay. *Effective Teaching of Reading,* 2nd ed. New York, N.Y.: David McKay Company, Inc., 1971.

McKee, Paul. "Vocabulary Development." *Thirty-Sixth Yearbook of the National Society for the Study of Education,* Part 1, pp. 277–302, Bloomington, Ill.: Public School Publishing Company, 1937.

Petty, Walter, Curtis Herold and Earline Stoll. *The State of Knowledge about the Teaching of Vocabulary,* pp. 7–24. Urbana, Ill.: National Council of Teachers of English, 1968.

Rivers, Wilga. *Teaching Foreign Language Skills.* Chicago, Ill.: The University of Chicago Press, 1968.

Sandstrom, Eleanor. *The Contributions of Foreign Language Learning to the Development of the Development of the Reading Skills.* FL 002 734. Philadelphia School District, Pennsylvania, 1970. ERIC ED 056 621. Arlington, VA.: ERIC Document Reproduction Service.

Tinker, Miles. *Teaching Elementary Reading.* New York, N.Y.: Appleton-Century-Crofts, Inc., 1952.

Story Dramatization in the Reading Center

by Andrea Wertheimer

When I introduced story dramatization in the reading center, I had two basic objectives in mind:

First, I wanted to motivate reluctant readers to read more through the avenues opened by drama.

Second, I hoped to help my students develop a sensitivity toward their classmates (as well as an understanding of both their classmates and characters in literature).

Perhaps the background of my teaching situation will help the reader begin to understand my reasons for using story dramatization in the reading center. The students in our school exist among a multitude of crisis situations. The school is located in Harlem among housing which is either overcrowded or abandoned. Extreme poverty is a reality with which my eighth graders are forced to cope. Hunger, death, eviction, rape and drugs are everyday situations and yet my students must survive. They need to develop and retain a positive view of themselves despite problems and an environment which are a national disgrace. For the many reasons which follow this introduction, I have found that story dramatization utilizes the close association between education and life in ways which help the student to succeed both inside and outside the classroom.

In one of the eleven different classes I teach, there are particularly disparate reading levels ranging from 2.0 to 6.0. After overhearing a few unusually insensitive remarks among my students regarding the reading levels of some of their classmates, I realized that I would have to try something to get this class "together." The students' outspoken rudeness towards one another was turning into a discipline problem which made classroom learning nearly impossible. At this point I needed to obtain a degree of discipline, not of the type which emphasizes silence or un-questioned obedience, but discipline which stresses mutual respect and understanding. I decided to try story dramatizations as a method of helping my students ''get into'' the attitudes and problems of their classmates via fictional characters and situations.

It has been said that,

''Drama'' means doing, acting things out rather than working on them in abstract and in private. When possible it is the truest form of learning, for it puts knowledge and understanding to their test in action.

In addition to Professor Dixon's explanation above in *Growth through English,* my reasons for using dramatizations in the reading center were that the class would have the opportunity to examine the social and psychological aspects of life-like situations from a distance. Drama offers distance just far enough to enable the student with a problem to remain anonymous to the class, while ''hitting home'' within him. Dramatic participation helps the student to get as close as possible to certain realities which he could not reach or would find too painful to reach or would at first hand. Finally, drama allowed me to focus on a specific problem in the classroom without hurting or pointing a finger at anyone.

For reluctant readers, in-class story dramatizations which are not audience-oriented may make students less self-conscious and more relaxed. They begin to use creative expression, develop a sense of confidence, and at times, employ their own imaginations to embellish a role. This occurs, more often when the teacher declines to act as critic. Through story dramatization many students discover for the first time the power and strength of words, and the changes in effect depending on how and when they are spoken. Words cease to become enemies, especially if any new or difficult vocabulary is taught beforehand.

MATERIALS

The materials which I used in this project were:

Ball, Jacqueline A., ed. *Read: The Magazine for Reading and English.* Connecticut: Xerox Corporation, 1974.
(This magazine is written on a 7.0–9.0 reading level. The plays may be correlated with a variety of topics taught in language arts. A recent issue [March 15, 1974] dealt with American speech. It contained a play about a girl moving from one city to another and the subsequent problems of understanding regional accents.)

Brodkin, Sylvia. *Close-Up: A Collection of Short Plays.* New York: Globe Book Co., 1970.

(This is a more sophisticated collection of plays with reading levels ranging from 7.0–9.0. Many of the plays are suitable for auditorium presentation.)

Celabush, Mel, ed. *Take 12/Action Plays*. New York: School Division of Scholastic Magazines, Inc., 1970.
(This is a collection of twelve plays dealing with contemporary adolescent problems at a reading level of 3.0–4.5. Most of the plays call for five to eight characters which is ideal for small group situations. This collection is excellent as an introduction for students who are inexperienced in role-playing or who are fearful of assuming a role.)

Celabush, Mel, ed. *Scope Play Anthologies*. New York: Scholastic Book Services, 1973.
(This is a collection of seven anthologies of the best plays from those appearing in *Scope* magazine. A free teaching guide is available when twenty or more copies of any one anthology are ordered. The reading level varies from 4.0–6.0.)

Robinson, Katherine, ed. *Scholastic Scope*. New York: School Division of Scholastic Magazines, Inc., 1974.
(Almost every issue of this weekly publication has a play suitable for classroom use. The reading level varies from 4.0–6.0. The settings of the plays are especially interesting. Recent issues have settings in Appalachia, the old West, and New York at the turn of the century, as well as contemporary urban and suburban communities. Occasionally an issue concentrates on one author or theme. A recent issue [March 7, 1974] dealt with O. Henry and his use of the surprise ending. If your school library orders *Scope*, the plays can be reproduced via thermofax or Xerox for classroom use.)

PROCEDURES

With the above problems and students in mind, I explained to the class that for the next few sessions we would put our usual reading lessons aside. We would each take parts or roles and do some plays in order to respond to one another with greater understanding. A few initial responses were: "I don't want no one watching me," "Plays are junk," and "You can't read anything good in class anyway." The class was very surprised that we were going to do plays about sickle-cell anemia, a girl dating an older boy, parents committing their son to a narcotics rehabilitation home and loyalty between friends. They agreed to give it a try as long as neither writing nor an audience was involved.

After discussing new vocabulary, choosing parts was the next step. Initially, I assigned the parts, attempting to distribute the roles fairly but keeping in mind that the play had to "move" or the class would become bored or distracted. After the first few plays I stepped out of the "director" role since some of the class members developed enough skill and understanding to almost take over the class.

Before actually doing the first play together, we had to discuss the importance of setting, scene and playing a role. We discussed the meaning of setting and scene by giving practical examples. For instance, the park, subway, apartment and school building are all different settings. The class realized that people act differently depending on where they are, so they decided to keep that in mind while playing their parts. Also a setting often zeros in on particular scenes. The setting of a play may be a school, but Scene I may take place in typing class, Scene II may take place in the lunch room and Scene III in the principal's office. People certainly act in a different way in each of the scenes we mentioned.

The next step was a difficult one. Some students had difficulty realizing that what they said or what was said to them as the parts were being played was not to be taken personally. It was mentioned that we could learn to understand and respond to the problems of others, but should not take the experiences we dramatized as mirrors of our own lives. We might, however, learn from situations that other people have had to face and see which alternative could be suitable for us. We did not have to agree with the characters or with the points of view of our classmates, but we should respect them.

So during the four weeks preceding spring recess we performed the dramatizations together. We used plays appearing in *Action/Take 12*, *Scope* and *Close-Up* already annotated in this article. At first many of the students felt self-conscious about following the stage directions. Eventually, many of the students grew comfortable enough to really get involved with their parts. They realistically attempted to sound like parents, excited teenagers or people filled with anger. Emotions were released in many instances but to constructive ends. The class enjoyed themselves while learning some things about self-expression, the problems of others, and a new and entertaining way to use their reading skills. At this point a few evaluative comments and suggestions are necessary in order to judge whether the drama project accomplished its objectives.

IN RETROSPECT

The first objective—that of motivating reluctant readers to read via story dramatizations—was accomplished quite successfully. Besides reading the plays assigned and/or freely chosen in class, many of the students borrowed other collections of plays from the class and school libraries. Many of the students have since read stories and tried to turn them into dramatizations for the class. This was an unintended result but nevertheless a welcome one. Perhaps some of these students can now go on to read material which cannot be dramatized without the negative feedback of the past.

Concerning the second objective, there are some positive signs that point to a heightened sense of understanding among many of the students. The very deficient readers responded more favorably and enthusiastically to the drama projects than to their individually-tailored basic skills lessons. They seemed to rise to the occasion and read with more ease and expression than they usually did. The more advanced readers displayed a degree of patience which was not in operation until the drama sequence began. When some of the students began to direct the plays themselves, they assigned parts to slower readers with the same fairness as to the more advanced readers in the class. Thus the slower readers were finally recognized by their peers as people, too. This project successfully brought together students with widely disparate reading levels as they accomplished a task both in a social and scholastic sense.

In addition, the students learned to listen to one another well enough to develop insight into themselves and others. Many times emotions reached a high-pitch, but the use of drama had developed their sense of perspective and point of view enough to allow them to at least respect one another's reasoning.

The dramatizations allowed some students to release such inner feelings as: guilt, rejection, personal resentment and fear, which are especially strong in adolescents. Through sensing the thoughts and feelings of others, they developed the ability to work and cooperate within a group.

Perhaps an interesting follow-up activity would involve the students in trying out their own original ideas—in written form first and later as a dramatization. This idea might be preceded by students writing dramatizations of stories already in print. The reading ability of some students may be improved by having them write scripts and read them.

Whatever form of drama you may choose, beware of one important point. The students must really "dig" the setting, problems and conflicts appearing in the drama. If some students are known to be too emotionally charged, a mystery story dramatization may provide a more successful beginning than a play with a family focus. Be selective in your choice of dramas, but remember that plays and situations which work for one group may be a dead-end for another group so come prepared with plenty of alternative selections. Also try the suggestions of the group and half of your motivation is already accomplished. Despite a few plays that did not work, my students in reading class developed more understanding towards one another, enjoyed themselves, and became increasingly motivated to read in the process!

Acting Out Language Skills

by Rose M. Feinberg

So often we look for ways to teach language skills other than drill and workbooks. I have found that children enjoy ''acting out'' language skills, and this can be done in many ways. A good approach is for the class to work in pantomime. At other times, small groups may perform, with guessing and responses coming from observers. Some activities can be done in pairs, with other pairs observing and responding. Often the same activity can be varied by using individuals, pairs, small groups, the whole class, or even two or more classes.

Adjectives When you are working with younger children, call this activity the idea that words describe.

Movement description of self—Children move in pantomime as if angry, bossy, sad, joyful. Other adjectives come from group.

Opening presents—As children open presents in imaginative pantomime, they take turns describing the gift. Only adjectives may be used. Example: ''It's soft, cuddly, black and white, intelligent. . . . '' Others guess what it might be.

Characters—In a brainstorming session, the group creates a group of characters, each described by a suitable adjective. Examples: mischievous little girl, jolly window washer, sly clerk. Select four characters from the list and present them in a skit. The adjectives should be discussed so characters can be portrayed accurately.

Adverbs For primary children, create a list of adverbs that they can refer to during the following activities.

Adverb mirror—Children stand in circles, four to six in a group. One person leads the group in the manner of the word called out by the teacher. The group moves exactly as the leader does. Directions may be to lead boldly, shyly, forcefully, eagerly, uncertainly, and so on.

What was the adverb?—One person leaves the room as the rest decide on an adverb. When the person is called in, he or she asks persons in the group to "perform" the adverb. Example: "Jerry, please run in the way the adverb describes." The person guesses, then asks other persons to perform actions, and continues until the adverb is guessed.

Alphabet letters The letters of the alphabet are displayed or written, for children to see the proper configuration. They reproduce some letters using glue, sandpaper, or yarn. Children hear, see, or touch a letter. Then they create it with their bodies. Or they can join in pairs or larger groups.

For drill in alphabetical order, movement words on cards are given to children, who arrange themselves in order using the movement on the card or by doing a movement relating to the word. Observers can tell if students are in correct alphabetical order.

Antonyms List words that are antonyms to use with younger children. Older children can create their own. From these lists, select one set of antonyms and act out the words. For example, one might stand and the other sit for: tall-short; high-low; up-down.

Capitalization As a sentence is read, children act in a specified way to indicate when a capital is needed. They might stand up, wave arms, jump. This would be a good reinforcement technique after capitalization has been introduced. Individual children could create sentences and direct group movements.

Classification Discuss categories of objects—things we ride, ways we move, articles in a house, school supplies, and so on. Then call out the category and ask children to perform any action that relates to it.

Compound words Brainstorm compound words and write them on cards. Each pair selects a card and acts out both parts. One person could pretend to be getting wet from the "rain," for example, while the other uses a "bow" to shoot an arrow. Observers put the two together to form the compound word. Card is shown to verify word.

Following directions An important side effect of these activities is added skill in listening.

Written commands or oral commands—Each person writes a simple command on a slip of paper—open a door, shovel snow. (Whisper the commands to younger children.) One person at a time obeys the imperative. The others wait until the person says "ready"; then tell what the command was. Variations include steps to follow in "how to do something." Observers tell the order of the commands, repeat the steps in pantomime, or do both.

Through an obstacle course—Items in the room are arranged in an obstacle course. One child directs how to go through the course while the other tries to follow the directions.

Homonyms List pairs of homonyms. Partners pick a pair, prepare a set of cards containing the homonyms, and act out one of them. Observers tell which person, for example, is acting out "stare" (looking through binoculars pantomime) and which is acting out "stair" (making walking motion). The correct spelling is shown. Older students write the spellings before being shown correct forms.

Intonation Take any word or phrase and ask children to say it in as many different ways as possible. Examples: Say "oh" as if you just got a present; as if someone kicked you; as if you just realized the answer.

Listening Acting out activities increases listening skills. Pairs of children listen for directions (see "Following Directions"), listen to each other's dialogue, listen to add to what's been said, and so on.

Main idea A group acts out a situation from something seen or written. Observers tell what idea is being depicted. Ideas could be written down and these ideas shared before the group tells original main idea.

Multiple-meaning words Many words have different meanings in different situations. Make lists of words that have multiple meanings (*fall* can mean a season or an action). In pairs or trios, children act out situations. Observers tell the meaning being acted out.

Nonverbal communication A gesture or body movement can tell many things.
Directions—In pairs, children give directions using gesture only—down, stop, come here, go there.
Body talk—Have different parts of the body communicate feelings. Examples: feet could show fear; hands show excitement; entire body could show waiting in line for a show, or to buy a ticket.

Nouns Use these and other activities to drill on different groups of nouns.
Emotions through pantomime—Situations are given verbally to half the group. The other half observe and write the emotions observed. These are discussed and listed. New situations are given to the other side. Observers note elation, excitement, exultation, happiness, disbelief, and so on. Example: "You just received a million dollars. Show how you feel."
Names of things—Showing an actual item, children tell all the different things something could be. Example: cloth could be shawl, tablecloth, headband, belt, sling, turban. Groups could create actions using these items.
Occupations—Children discuss various jobs, then act one out. Observers tell the name of the occupation. Picture or word clues can be used with younger children.

Prepositions When first working with prepositions, create a class list to refer to.

Where am I?—Someone starts an action that takes place in a specific area. Example: swinging on the playground. As others guess the action, they do others appropriate to the place. Continue until all realize they are "on the playground."

When is it?—Each person pantomimes an action taking place at a certain time—in the morning, during the afternoon, or at night. Older students could use specific times—arising at seven o'clock, eating at five o'clock, and so on.

Where did I go?—Children are given prepositional phrases to act out. Observers tell where the person went. Example: under the flag.

Through an obstacle course—Specific directions are under "Following Directions." When giving and repeating directions, children make prepositions clear. Example: "Go over the chair, around the table, under the banner, over the paper."

Pronouns Pupils write situations on cards using pronouns; a group of three or four acts out the situation. Observers describe the situation, using pronouns in responses. Example: they went shopping and met their friends. Cards with pronouns and situations could be matched to create new acting-out situations.

Punctuation Children can create agreed-upon body shapes for each punctuation mark. Large word cards arranged in sentences are placed on the floor. Punctuation is created by children's bodies at correct places. Other observers check floor arrangement.

Sentences Give extended drill on one kind of sentence before moving to the next type.

Commands or imperatives—Directions are under "Following Directions." As children observe commands acted out, they write the sentence as an imperative—"Close the door."

Question or interrogative—By questioning, children guess an action done. They can ask, "Did you shovel coal?"

Statement—Children are given a statement to act out. Others guess the action pantomimed and state it in a complete sentence. "You were riding a horse."

Sequence—Sequence is reinforced as children listen for order to reenact a story. For a second activity, give a sequence of events which children follow. Example: Run forward, hop three times, pick up a hat, and go to the center. Also see "Following Directions."

Spelling The words used in spelling activities are dependent, of course, on the group's needs and abilities.

Body spelling—Children create words with their bodies. Teams can be used with captains directing members into proper arrangement from spelling cards.

Word families—Children make lists of words which have the same endings: -old, -ate, -ot, -an, -ee, and so on. A group chooses a word family to act out. Others observe and write down the words.

Tenses Present, past, and future signs are made. Children act as directed, or create their own actions. As a person does an action standing under *present* sign, observers guess, "You are walking up stairs;" under *past* sign, "You walked up stairs"; under *future* sign, "You will walk up stairs."

Children can write sentences on slips of paper using various tenses; others act them out standing under the correct sign.

Verbs Before using these activities, take time to brainstorm a long class list of verbs—not to refer to so much as to get pupils to thinking what makes a verb.

Do the action—One child at a time does an action suggested on a slip of paper, by a picture, or as he imagines one. Observers list possible verbs being demonstrated. This could be either oral or written.

Change the action—Create a sentence and change the verb each time someone acts it out. This demonstrates the power of verbs in a sentence and expands verb vocabulary of children. Example: The boy hobbled to the tent; shuffled; trudged.

Vocabulary Have the children learn meanings of difficult words by becoming these words. Example: apparitions flying about.

Written expression Creative writing can take place at every level.

Trapped somewhere—Various locations are suggested in a brainstorming session. Children can pretend to be normal size, large, or tiny, and be trapped in one of the places. In pantomime, children show where they are, then escape. This is an excellent vehicle for writing about being trapped and the feelings involved.

What happened?—Children in turn put an expression on their faces for others to observe. Observers decide on a situation which might cause this expression. Ideas are shared, and person tells original situation. These ideas are used for story starters or general story ideas.

Who could that be?—One person decides on a character. Without being seen, the person conveys a situation or character type by a sound effect. This could be a way of knocking, or walking, and so on. Observers write ideas, and character tells what he was trying to portray. These become ideas for writing.

Act out written stories—An incentive for writing is the knowledge that their story or play will be acted out. Children can work in groups to create stories. After hearing them, a child is selected to act one out.

Movement stories—A group brainstorms different places to go, ways to walk, adventures to have. The teacher or a student creates a story with the class using the ideas given. The movement story is experienced in pantomime as it is told.

There are so many more acting-out activities which involve language skills. Children will often suggest ideas. Keep in mind that as children create and act out situations, and improvise dialogue and gesture, they are refining their communication skills. Using acting out to reinforce skills in language is a worthwhile approach to learning.

PART III
Literature and Theater

Introductory Comments

Drama provides an opportunity for students to inspect and analyze literature at their own emotional and intellectual levels. The words virtually come alive when enacted and become much more than printed letters on a page.

"Literature presented through various dramatic techniques offers students an opportunity for a creative exchange of ideas that aids in developing the whole person," state Catherine O'Shea and Margaret Egan in their article, "A Primer of Drama Techniques for Teaching Literature." Because both women are teachers, the devices they present have been tested in the classroom; and their suggestions include pantomime, improvisation, extrapolation, role playing, and other techniques.

"Theater in the Classroom" by Michael and Pamela Malkin also includes structured lessons. The authors' activities place an emphasis on communicating and helping the students to learn to work together.

Jonathan Potter utilizes an ancient approach to add a spark to his student productions: "Liven Up Your Student Dramatics with Commedia dell' Arte" illustrates ways in which the vitality of the Commedia can increase student interest and generate enthusiasm.

"Shakespeare for the Fun of It" by Libby Colman relates her experiences in sharing *The Tempest* with elementary children, and Patrick Groff explores the intriguing approaches provided with "Readers Theater by Children." He demonstrates that this uncomplicated activity can provide a stimulus for improving reading skills and for encouraging students to examine a work's tone, theme, and mood.

A Primer of Drama Techniques for Teaching Literature

by Catherine O'Shea and Margaret Egan

"Teacher, teacher, *show* me what you mean." It is possible for students on the threshold of the 1980s to learn and to enjoy literature, to work diligently, to complain righteously, and yet to find wonder in exploring and discovering the ideas and values of another time.

Literature presented in a dramatic fashion does just this. It provides students with a technicolor approach to a black and white problem. Dramatic techniques place the young actors in situations which require them to respond spontaneously and objectively. Frequently these unstudied responses are not in accord with their usual manner of "acting." Fictional dramatic situations provide students with an opportunity to offer insights and to state viewpoints that they were not previously aware of holding.

Every English teacher knows that paradoxes not only fascinate students but also hold up truths for their viewing. Watch their faces as they become aware that "pain brings joy," "happiness causes tears," and that "death holds life." This way of looking at reality can be achieved in an atmosphere of interested inquiry, interaction, and hard work. Enthusiastic, exciting literature classes are a possibility!

Through the study of literature in a junior/senior high program, students often for the first time begin to reflect seriously and see ways to respond to what they feel within themselves. A teacher must present opportunities for students to develop personal insights, creative bents, and to fashion attainable hopes.

Simulated experiences enliven ponderous reading material and bring it into a perspective that students can understand. Dramatic action stimulates and fosters their desire to share poetry, mythology, short stories, novels, and plays that have been transformed into experiential situations which answer the questions: *Who am I? What are my roots? Where am I going? What will I become?*

Teaching devices that place students in action are needed in every literature class today. To help answer the request, ''Teacher, teacher, show me,'' we present this primer of dramatic approaches to literature:

PANTOMIME

Pantomime is one of the oldest forms of acting, consisting of a sequence of facial expressions, gestures, hand and body movements that have been observed from life and are imaginatively used by actors to tell something pertinent about: character, situation, locale, and atmosphere.

Warm-Up Activities

Let all or any student who wishes demonstrate a simple ''pantomime.''

1. Pretend that you are getting dressed for a ''party.'' It can be any kind of party. If you wish, have another student assist you in the pantomime.
2. Pretend that you are picking up a dead mouse from the floor; emphasize your distaste for this task.
3. Pretend that you are watching a horror movie in a crowded theater.
4. Pretend that you are a clown blowing up a balloon, or that you are trying to catch a butterfly.

Application to Literature: *Aesop's Fables*

Select a favorite fable that you think the group will find amusing. Using only facial, hand and body movements, pretend that you are the character(s). Convey the story of the fable stressing the main conflict and the end results that illustrate the moral. (If needed ask another student to assist you.)

Other Suggestions

1. O. Henry's ''Ransom of Red Chief''
2. Shakespeare's *Hamlet*—Act III, Scene II—The ''dumb show'' of the ''Mouse Trap''

Experience Gained/Insights Received

—To improve body coordination and control.

—To lessen ''self consciousness'' when performing group activities.

—To learn that to work closely with others requires support and mutual dependence.

—To develop an individual's abilities to create a dramatic situation, a fictional characterization.

—To become more observant about people's behavior and mannerisms in everyday situations.

—To familiarize students with an early form of literature: fables, myths, etc., which depict the forces of good and evil, right and wrong.

—To make students more aware of the universal truths that are common to all men, to help them recognize and respond to them.

IMPROVISATION

Improvisation is the ability to create a very brief plot or story, implementing it with dialogue that is not planned or rehearsed.

Warm-Up Activities

Select a topic to which everyone can relate in some way.

Where were you when the lights went out?

1. ''Brainstorm'' (Have each student call out words or phrases that fit the problem. Students will react to the ideas of others spontaneously. This technique starts a ''chain reaction'' of thoughts to flow.)
   a. Have two students record the ideas that are called out.
   b. Students will have a list of words and phrases which they can employ in an improvisation.
2. ''Newspaper and Magazine Ads''
   a. In class tell each group to cut out about 10 ''ads'' that catch their imaginations.
   b. Next, tell each group that they are to use these ads in the improvised skit.
   c. Give each group 20 minutes to put some logical sequence of order into the materials they have selected. Each ad must in some sensible fashion lead into the next one.

    d. Students may use the words of the ad as part of their dialogue. If needed, a sentence or two may be added to help make logical connections.

    e. The actions and the words of the improvisation should be based on the ideas students received from the ads.

3. Create a scene in which only *one word* of dialogue may be used.

Application to Literature: Roman-Greek Myths

    Keep the same characters as the original myth but improvise the main conflict to fit a modern day issue. Each student must be familiar with the original myth. Reading it aloud in class is one way to be sure that all know the story. The group should discuss and agree upon the modern day issue they wish to expose. Each student should decide for him/herself before going on stage—*Who he/she is, what he/she is doing and why.*

    The response that each student gives will result in some very innovative and creative ideas which will be both interesting and exciting for their audience.

Other Suggestions

1. Poetry—''Richard Cory'' by Robinson
2. Short Story—''A Piece of String'' by Chekov
3. Current Newspaper or Magazine Articles

Experience Gained/Insights Received

—To increase spontaneity and creativity.

—To have students become aware of modern social issues.

—To provide a medium in which students can respond to relevant issues.

—To make students more sensitive to the changing feelings and attitudes of the other actors in the scene.

—To have students gain a deeper understanding of conflict and characterization in literature.

EXTRAPOLATION/EXPANDING A CHARACTER

Extrapolation or expanding a character is the extension of what is known about a character to what one could know if he/she were a real person.

Warm-Up Activities

1. *"What if"* statements—an excellent means of extending feelings and insights into a character's personality:
   a. What if Romeo and Juliet did not have the support and sympathy of Friar Lawrence?
   b. What if the Count of Monte Cristo had met a notorious gang leader in the Chateau instead of the old priest?
   c. What if the glass slipper had fit Cinderella's stepsister?
2. *"If I were"* statements give students the experience of extending his/her personal reactions to fictitious situations:
   a. If I were Anne Frank, would I have recorded the intimate details of my affection for Peter?
   b. If I were Homer in the novel *The Human Comedy,* how would I have responded to delivering the telegram to Mrs. Sandoval that told of her son's death in the war?

Application to Literature: Fairy Tales

Choose one of Hans Christian Anderson's tales that appeals to you. (Remember that fairy tales generally include: an element of the supernatural, an unsurmountable obstacle that the hero must overcome, good that always triumphs over evil in the end.)

Choose a character with whom you can identify and create for that character a dual personality by extrapolating a new response to the dilemma:

- Cinderella's predicament
- Snow White's plight
- The quandary of The Emperor Who Had No Clothes

Experience Gained/Insights Received

—To expose students to "fairy tales," one of the most fanciful and creative story forms, to entertain an audience and show that hope is an essential ingredient for man in solving life's problems.

—To provide students with a new insight into characterization.

—To encourage students to use their personal insights in responding to life's situations.

—To have students penetrate further into character analysis.

—To have students identify with feelings that are not necessarily their own.

—To create an empathy and an objectivity in looking at various situations.

ROLE PLAYING

Role playing is another means of self-revelation that involves students physically and verbally to interpret another's ideas.

Warm-Up Activities

"Come Follow Me." Use a full length mirror or have students face each other. One student becomes the *leader* and initiates the actions that the other student, *reflection,* must mirror; e.g.—eating a lemon, lighting a candle.

Application to Literature: Novels

Choose a scene from Steinbeck's *The Pearl*; e.g., the conversation between the doctor and Juan.

1. Reread the episode in order for each student to understand the atmosphere and conflict of the scene.
2. Ask each student to jot down ideas about one character he/she chooses to role play.
3. How would each one change the character's word and actions?
4. Now students are ready to act out the scene with the changes they suggested.

Other Suggestions

Scenes from any of the following: *To Kill A Mockingbird, The Glass Menagerie, The Autobiography of Miss Jane Pitman* or any TV show.

Experience Gained/Insights Received

—To have students meet their own feelings of outrage, anger, and sympathy, etc., in controlled situations.
—To have students respond to these emotions objectively or not so objectively as the case may be.
—To help students to come in touch with the feelings of the characters in the literary works studied.
—To help students realize that extenuating circumstances do affect one's reactions.

READER'S THEATER

Reader's theater is a performance of a dramatic reading of a poem, novel, play, or short story. No sets are used. Actors must attempt verbally to communicate as honestly as possible an author's ideas, feelings, and intentions to the audience.

Warm-Up Activities

1. Use a tape for each of the following activities:
   a. Speak a simple command to someone near you. Repeat the same command to another at a distance. Be aware of the change in voice and the reaction to the command in both instances.
   b. Ask a question.
   c. Give an exclamation of surprise, shock, pain.
2. Read a short selection from a poem. Underline the words that you think hold the emotion of the poem. Read the poem aloud stressing those words you have underlined.

Application to Literature: Poetry

"The Death of a Hired Man"—Robert Frost

1. Let each member of the group assume the role of a character, including that of the narrator.
2. Prepare a dramatic reading of the poem as you feel it is meant to be interpreted.
3. The effectiveness of the performance depends on the ability of the readers to look at the audience 80% of the time, to interpret and emphasize important ideas in a dramatic way, and to control the rate of delivery. Gestures that emphasize or communicate an idea more fully may be employed.

Other Suggestions

T. S. Eliot's "Cocktail Party," Robert Browning's "My Last Duchess," Shakespeare's soliloquies.

Experience Gained/Insights Received

—To encourage students to actualize the poem.
—To have students realize that voice reveals several important points about a stage character: his background, educational level, social class, occupation, age, emotional and physical conditions.

—To emphasize that clear pronunciation and varied inflections of the voice communicate emotions, thoughts, and personality.

—To have students learn to alter and control their voices according to the physical traits of the one they portray.

LIVE STAGE OR "GLOBE THEATER REVISITED"

Live stage is a performance that provides a workshop for students which gives them an opportunity to use a variety of artistic talent at their disposal.

Warm-Up Activities

1. The oral reading of lines of poems, lines from a play that show particular emotion in order to improve control.
2. Review "improvisational" techniques . . . to improve gesture and body control.

Application to Literature: Plays

Sorry, Wrong Number
Twelve Angry Men
Raisin in the Sun

Select a scene from a play that appeals to the group.

1. Choose a director, stage manager.
2. Assign character roles after tryouts.
3. Read the script aloud together in order to come to a consensus as to the theme of the play.
4. Have students decide whether or not they want to use the ideas of the "conventional theater" (memorizing lines and dramatizing the scene as it is) or adapt the scene to another medium—TV, radio, etc.

Experience Gained/Insights Received

—To provide students with a critical audience.

—To have students discover how characterization is revealed in a play by:
  • words that the character speaks
  • actions/mannerisms the character displays
  • what other people say about the character
  • what the character thinks aloud

—To show students how people judge others in a fictional situation and also in real life.

"EXCLUSIVELY OURS"

"Exclusively ours" is an opportunity that gives students a chance to write an original script that can be produced and performed in front of an audience.

Warm-Up Activities

1. Read a poem dramatically; endeavor to show emotion in your voice, eyes, and face. Review technique [for] Reader's Theater.
2. Read action poems. Ask another group of students to move and gesture with their bodies to portray the meaning of the poem as it is read. Review technique [for] Pantomime.
3. Listen to music. March, sway, etc., to express the feelings the music conveys.

Application to Literature: Short Stories

O. Henry's:
"Gift of the Magi"
"After Twenty Years"
"Retrieved Reformation"

1. Read the story together aloud. Each student may select a character that he/she can best portray.
2. After reading the story, discuss the main theme, conflict, etc. Change the "narration" form of the story into "dialogue" for each character. This is a challenging task. Work in groups of two since advanced writing skills are required.
3. If a narrator is needed to supply additional information: setting, background, etc., include one.
4. Select a director, stage manager, etc.
5. Practice the script for a class presentation.

Experience Gained/Insights Received

—To develop ways of handling problem situations that arise from:
  • student actors

- technical difficulties
- "red tape" that accompanies all of life

—To develop individual talents: writing and acting/costuming, etc.

—To expose students to both the personal satisfaction and the frustrations that come from being part of an original production.

—To develop a sensitivity to others; to learn to respect their ideas, their suggestions.

—To develop the ability to accept both public praise and criticism in a positive constructive way.

The knowledgeable teacher will utilize drama as an important aspect of the curriculum. Whether the syllabus calls for the reading of the ancient myths, or the short stories of de Maupassant, whether students are required to read a twentieth century Robert Frost or a nineteenth century Emily Dickinson—all will be transported to the present time via skits, taped interviews, impromptu role playing, soliloquies, etc. Arduous reading assignments will take on new forms that will interest, entertain, and teach students that literature is not dead, but alive and well.

Literature presented through various dramatic techniques offers students an opportunity for a creative exchange of ideas that aids in developing the whole person. Students will not only read literature but come to a deeper understanding of why authors and poets had to express their feelings. Students will recognize their own emotions, doubts, fears, and hopes and will be offered opportunities to express them and test them with their peers.

A dramatic approach to literature improves writing skills, sharpens insights, develops initiative, disciplines mind and body, prepares students to organize and present their ideas, and hopefully helps them to find acceptance and a sense of achievement. Idealistic? Yes! Possible? Yes!

Theater in the Classroom, Part I

by Michael and Pamela Malkin

A unit on theater arts related to art and music classes has a place in every classroom. It helps to develop communication skills, can relate to other curriculum areas, builds self-confidence and self-discipline and can be tremendously exciting for youngsters.

What is currently popular as "creative dramatics" goes under many guises. It often turns up as vaguely defined exercises in role playing and improvisation. This can be misleading to students who are convinced that they are learning about theater when, in fact, they are not.

The group of structured lessons described in this article includes improvisatory activities in a unit that does develop the craft, creativity and art of the theater. The children are involved in exercises that incorporate six basic principles of theater and creative drama: *imagination, concentration, observation, characterization, improvisation* and *rhythm*.

SPECIFIC GOALS

One major difference between carefully structured theater lessons and role-playing games is that the theater activities are geared to performance before an audience. Even if a play or skit is not staged formally, there are likely to be some students watching.

The presence of an audience is a strong motivating factor in working toward the four goals of our theater unit: First, each child will develop the confidence to perform in front of others, without inhibitions or fear. Second, each child will learn that acting is not showing off, that it is a skill involving the recreation of believable characters and situations, plus the ability to communicate thoughts and feelings to others. Our emphasis on communication differs slightly from the approach that stresses self-expression. Third, each student will learn to control his or her characterization as well as the dramatic situation, in order to build a sequence of events that has a discernible beginning, middle and end. Finally, the students will develop a strong sense of cooperation and teamwork. They will learn how to work together to keep the action moving along smoothly.

Our theater unit is roughly designed to fit a schedule of three one-hour classes a week for 12 weeks. This article covers the imagination and concentration activities; next month there will be follow-up lessons, focusing on observation, characterization, improvisation and rhythm. All the activities are models for similar ones you'll develop.

IMAGINATION

Dramatic Imaginings

We find that most children between six and 11 do not have to be "taught" to pretend or imagine. However, they often do need training in how to communicate their imaginings to others, making them *dramatic* imaginings.

In order to develop an awareness of this kind of communication, we ask our students to create a number of imaginary situations that involve elementary pantomime and role playing. This kind of experience can be made much more vivid by asking the students a number of goal-directed questions.

These questions are in no way tests or value judgments but serve to help the children clarify the details of each imaginary situation. Using your own judgment, ask questions while and after the students perform.

The following are three situations, typical of the kind we ask our students to imagine, and some of the questions we ask them.

Walking a tightrope. How high up are you? Is there a safety net? Is this your first time on a tightrope? How tightly is the rope strung? Are you indoors or outdoors? If you are outdoors, is there any wind? Are you afraid? How narrow is the rope? How easily do you keep your balance?

Walking through tall grass. How tall is the grass? Is it wet or dry? How thick is it? Are there animals or insects in the grass? Are you enjoying yourself? Are you trying to find someone? Are you running from someone?

Walking through mud. Is the mud warm or cold? How deep is it? Do you have shoes on? Are you enjoying walking through the mud or do you want to get out of it?

Pretend Games

Imaginary group games help your students communicate and cooperate with the other members of a theatrical group. Begin with something simple like two people playing catch with an imaginary ball or frisbee. You might work up to something as complex as a complete game of baseball in which all of the props, including the ball and bat, are imaginary. Tennis, football, basketball or any game the kids are interested in can be a good basis for small dramas.

Appropriate goal-directed questions might include: Does everyone know who has the ball? Is everyone playing with the same size ball? When the ball is thrown or hit, does everyone know in what direction and how fast it's going?

During these games, let the students talk to one another about their activity if they wish. But be sure to discourage them from *narrating* or describing, rather than *playing* or performing the action of the games. For example, they shouldn't say: "Johnny, I'm going to throw this at you. It's going to be a fast ball. Oops, I threw it over your head. No, it's not there."

Story Pantomimes

In this lesson, individual students pantomime their interpretations of very short stories as you are telling them. Although the complexity of the narratives will vary according to the age and sophistication of your students, keep them simple and clear. Be sure each depicts a progression of emotionally charged actions.

For example: "You are walking home after having stayed late at school. The sun has gone down, and it's cold and dark. But you're not in a hurry because you have a bad report card that you don't want to show to your parents. You take a detour through some woods, and you suddenly realize that it's completely dark. You can't even see the path. You realize that you've lost your way, so you sit down by a tree and try to calm yourself. You look around and see a faint light in the distance. Carefully, you pick your way through the woods using the light as a marker. You're out of the woods, and you start to run towards the light. It's the house of a friend. You're safe!"

CONCENTRATION

The ability to focus all attention and energy on a specific set of goals is as important to theater arts as it is to athletics and such other performing arts as dance and music.

The Mirror Exercise

This is perhaps the best-known, the most used and the least understood activity related to creative dramatics and actor training. Students are paired and told to move together as though they were mirroring one another's actions. Their goal is to make it impossible for an observer to pick out the "follower" and "leader," *not* for one to follow the other's actions or take turns imitating one another.

This entails not only a great deal of concentration on the part of the students but also a basic understanding of the nature of movement. Does one action flow smoothly into the next? Do both participants always have a sense of what they are going to do next? Do the actions have a rhythm?

What Can You Hear?

A good, short, change-of-pace activity to go with the mirror game, this exercise concentrates on sounds in the classroom. Can you hear the heating system? Do the lights buzz? Is the clock ticking? Can you hear yourself or others breathing? What can you hear?

The Lost Object

Ask the children to imagine they have lost a very valuable object. Have them concentrate on looking for it. Ask such questions as: Is there a method to your search? When and where did you last have it? What have you done since then? Does this object mean a great deal to you? Is it valuable? Do you want other people—or another person, in particular—to know that it's lost? Did it belong to you? Are you afraid that someone else will find it first? Have you searched everywhere?

Once again, it is best if the action is pantomimed, because many students will have a perfectly natural tendency to describe rather than to show what they are feeling. This and similar exercises will help students understand that there is more to seemingly simple actions and emotions than they had thought.

The Football Game

Tell the children you will narrate a football game. If possible bring in a recording of someone announcing an actual game. Have each person in the class choose a side before you begin and root for one of the teams as you narrate. After the narration, ask: Were you really pleased or were you only trying to *show* that you were pleased? Were you really disappointed or were you only trying to show that you were disappointed? Did you react only to the action of the game or did you express your feelings before or after some of the plays, too?

The Arithmetic Problem

Give one child a simple arithmetic problem to solve in his or her head. Have the other students try to distract the one who is ''it' without using physical force. See how many solve their problem.

Another similar exercise asks a student to try to make a paper airplane, while the others do something distracting. Undoubtedly you will think of other examples. *Improvisation for the Theater* by Viola Spolin (Northwestern University Press) is a rich source of ideas for developing concentration.

Theater in the Classroom, Part II

by Michael and Pamela Malkin

OBSERVATION

It is difficult to create or recreate characters and situations without a reservoir of detailed information. The actor must be able to both *see* and *remember* specific things about people, things and events.

Do you or your students know the exact number of steps on the front porch of your home? Can the children remember what their brother or sister or mother was wearing this morning? In fact, can they, without looking, tell you what color socks they are wearing? These kinds of questions show the children how easy it is to go through a day seeing an extraordinary number of things but observing very few of them. Here are three activities that increase powers of observation.

1. *Observing is not staring.* Have pairs of students observe each other for one minute. Then have them face away and answer such questions as: Did the child's shirt have pockets? What color are his or her eyes?

2. *The draped tray.* Place several different small objects (a thimble, a pencil, a spoon, etc.) on a tray and cover it with a cloth. Now show it for 15 seconds or less. Cover the tray again. Ask the students to try to remember what was on it. Since any number of objects can be used, start with a few simple ones and increase the number and complexity gradually. This game helps develop the skills of observing and remembering.

3. *Move as I move.* Ask your students to try to duplicate your movements as you move your body into various positions.

CHARACTERIZATION

When children learn to concentrate on certain parts of their bodies, it helps them forget themselves and gives them the flexibility to become another character much more easily. Try the following two exercises.

1. *What kind of person.* Ask the children to try to concentrate on various parts of their faces in order to become, for example, a "nose person," a "forehead person," a "chin person." [For more detail on these activities look at "Facing a Character," by Malkin in the May, 1974, *Dramatics.*] Ask such questions as: What different kinds of people can you make from your forehead person? How quickly can you change from being a forehead person to a nose person? How do you feel when you become a chin person? How would your chin person sweep the floor or eat soup?

2. *Interaction.* Have a "forehead person" and a "chin person" come into a room where there is only one chair. Each wants the other to sit down in it. The students may speak if they want.

Or try these situations. A "nose person" and a "left ear" person are entering or exiting through a door. Each wants the other to go first. A "left eye" person and a "right ear" person are introduced to one another for the first time.

IMPROVISATION

By now, your students are ready to make up and act out short, simple stories complete with dialogue. Explain that improvisation is an important part of most rehearsal procedures. In the theater, improvisations are not simply fun, role-playing exercises. Instead they enable actors and actresses to train themselves to answer such questions as "How do I cross to the desk?" or "How do I say this line?"

A useful but widely different approach to improvisation is discussed in Viola Spolin's *Improvisation for the Theater* (Northwestern University Press). Two suggestions follow, but there are many ways to handle improvisations. Have students work in groups of three or more with approximately 20 minutes to prepare their scene. Follow up with a session of constructive criticism.

1. *Situations.* Have your students improvise brief incidents, such as starting up a baseball game, fixing a broken bicycle, taking care of unruly children or getting lost in the woods.

2. *Objects.* Have the students find such imagined objects as an old toy, a trunk, an old photograph album, a microscope, a mirror, an old rowboat.

Relevant questions to ask in discussions after each performance are: Did the actors listen to one another? Did the actors' words and actions develop from moment to moment? Did the the improvisation have a beginning, a middle and an end? Did the way the actors moved correspond with what they said? Did the actors believe in what they were doing? Did the audience?

TEMPO RHYTHM IN MOVEMENT AND SPEECH

One of the most difficult lessons for student actors to learn is how to vary tempo and rhythm in movement and speech. A complete discussion of this topic can be found in Constantin Stanislavski's book, *Building a Character* (trans. by Elizabeth R. Hapgood, Theater Arts Books, N.Y., N.Y.).

1. *Change the tempo*. Bring in a metronome and set it to a particular beat. Ask a student group to act out one of its previously performed improvisations to a rhythm determined by the ticking of the metronome. Then halve the beat and have the students perform their scene to the new rhythm. Now double the original beat.

It is important that the students realize that the rhythm of the scene is altered, not necessarily the speed of line delivery. Rather than speaking or moving very slowly or quickly, they should concentrate on varying the tempo of their characters and their scenes.

Most students find this exercise challenging and exciting. The follow-up discussion should focus on the effects of tempo rhythm on all the elements of the improvisation. What happened to your characters? How did a particular moment seem to change when the tempo did? How did changes affect the general mood?

2. *Quick change*. During this exercise, vary the beat of the metronome several times during a performance of each improvisation. Did the actors really respond to the new beats? Did everyone respond at the same time? Did everyone respond to each change in the same way? How did changes in tempo rhythm affect the improvisation?

3. *Group performances*. Give groups of two or three students a chance to prepare either their own original improvisations or scenes from play-scripts for studio performance, using no costumes and minimal props. As they rehearse, encourage them to keep in mind everything they have learned thus far. Your students will both want and need a substantial amount of time to prepare. For a five- to ten-minute scene, a three-hour rehearsal is not excessive, and some older students may want even more time. Each scene or improvisation should be critiqued by the rest of the class immediately after it is performed.

Many suitable playscripts for children can be obtained from publishers whose names and addresses are listed under the section ''Play Publishers'' in *Witer's Market* . . . (ed. Jane Koester and Rose Adkins, Writer's Digest, Cincinnati, Ohio).

THE PLAY

After you have completed all the exercises, you can reinforce and tie them together by directing the class through the four- or five-week process of rehearsing and peforming a suitable one-act or even full-length play.

In practice, creative drama teachers sometimes put too much emphasis on the often ill-defined word ''creative'' and too little emphasis on drama or theater. We feel that training in theatrical performance techniques should be a primary goal of creative-drama exercises and the exercises given should get your kids excited about ''the theater.''

Liven Up Your Student Dramatics with Commedia Dell' Arte

by Jonathan Potter

How many times have you watched student actors recite their lines without any awareness of themselves as characters or of the other characters on the stage? This happened in dozens of my junior high and high school productions, and I struggled for a way to overcome it. I tried theater games based on material in Viola Spolin's book *Improvisations for the Theater*. The kids enjoyed doing them and did learn some basic theatrical skills as a result, but they had trouble seeing the connection between the games and putting on a show that their friends and relatives would see and admire.

Ah yes, admiration! Parents and relatives gushing things like " . . . learning those lines . . . what a lot of work! Wasn't Suzy marvelous!" But there was always that nagging question in my mind: If the audience notices the students who are doing the acting rather than the characters they are portraying, how successful was the stage production?

In an effort to conduct a play in which the audience would perceive the dialogue as speech between characters—as they're supposed to—and not as "lines," I tried using the Commedia dell' Arte. The results were so gratifying, both for me and the students, that I recommend this approach for anyone who is involved in student plays or in any teaching of dramatics.

What is this magical type of theater? Its origins are buried deep in the past. Between the productions of Greek tragedies, for example, bawdy interludes of physical comedy were staged. The Romans, who didn't particularly enjoy tragedy when there was something more sensational to watch, preferred raucous comedy to the static action and psychological tension of Greek tragedy. Roman comedy was usually acted by slaves, and pandered to the lowest and coarsest taste. Some of it survives today in the scripts of Plautus and Terence.

Because of its animal vitality, the Commedia persisted, particularly in Italy, even after the Roman Catholic Church had discouraged theater in the rest of the Western world. In time, the form was altered, and eventually the Commedia disappeared in the late eighteenth century—transformed into comic opera and Punch and Judy shows, solidified by Goldoni and Moliere into printed scripts, and ultimately overcome by the increasing public desire for elaborate, spectacular and elegant theater settings. What's left is a large number of scenarios (mostly in Italian or French, and untranslated), a rich legacy of stock characters, and an idea.

The idea is as simple as it is ancient. Given characters and a plot, actors create their own play. Most Commedia troupes were composed of players who had specialized in one particular character (Old Man, Bully, Rascally Servant, Young Lover), with younger actors often "inheriting" their roles from older relatives. Since the characters were already set, young Commedia players who grew up in the tradition had only to learn the new scenarios. (Often even that wasn't necessary because the scenario was posted behind the scenes for any actor who couldn't remember what came next.) Dialogue was created on the spot to meet the needs of the scene and to suit the immediate temper of the audience.

The stock characters are admirably listed in either of two standard works: *The Italian Comedy* by Pierre Louis Duchartre (Dover. . .) and *The Commedia dell' Arte* by Giacomo Oreglia (Hill and Wang. . .)— both in paperback. You don't absolutely need these references, but it's fun to teach a little tradition and history along with the show. My students like it, and usually find in these books connections with their characters that I have overlooked or discounted. And the profusion of illustrations in both books makes costuming and makeup research a breeze.

After tryouts (or assigning roles), begin immediately—the first day— working through the scenario you have chosen. You may find, to your dismay, that the first rehearsal will be very short. Don't despair. Illustrate.

Illustration is the surest way to successful direction of a Commedia. If you, as director, can assume a role and play a scene against the others in the cast, your ideas will be eagerly seized upon and used by your young actors. Once they have caught the spirit, rehearsals will grow longer and longer. When they reach the time limit you have set for your show—most Commedia plays are best at 60 to 90 minutes—begin asking the students what they think is boring and what isn't. (Or you can just call "next point" as a signal that a scene or bit has run too long, but get your students used to side-coaching first or they will just stop the action.)

Discussions after each act—*discussions,* not lectures—will open the actors to new ideas from each other. This is where things get exciting. The actors begin to feed each other opportunities and ideas, and the whole, rich, imaginative outpouring will surprise and delight you. Your actors will be using their brains and imaginations on stage, instead of being robots reproducing a playwright's limited concept and a single director's ideas.

As the show begins to jell, introduce the matter of audiences and the limits of taste. Your acting students—some of them, anyway—are likely to be swept away at times by their new freedom (or perhaps it is the old bawdy spirit of Commedia lifting its head). At any rate, ask them to do a rehearsal of the same scenario but aimed at small children, then one aimed at their parents. That should generate some interesting discussion of appropriate material. And if you're like me, it will also open your eyes to the acting skills your students have acquired.

As far as sets, lights, costumes and makeup are concerned, the rule for the Commedia is, "Keep It Simple."

The Commedia set I have developed is a street scene, since that's where most of our scenarios take place (for centuries, the Commedia was performed outside at fairs and marketplaces). Avoid using flats unless you are committed to them. I prefer scenes painted on muslin and attached to two pieces of closet pole so they can be rolled up when not in use. The top pole is attached to a wooden stand, making set-up time for a performance a matter of two minutes. (This is particularly useful if your rehearsal space is a corner of your classroom, a piece of the cafeteria, or a chunk of gym. It is also excellent for touring the show.) In several of the Commedias I have produced, the actors entered carrying the scenery and set it up themselves, while musicians played period music. If you are really strapped for cash, you might get away with using no scenery at all, but young actors generally feel more comfortable with something to play against.

Costuming and makeup are crucial to the success of the Commedia. For one thing, they make the actors more secure in their roles. They also set the audience's ideas clearly into a time frame and mood. The traditional Commedia male characters, with the exception of the Lovers, all had particular costumes, even to the color of the cloak (consult Duchartre or Oreglia for more details). Makeup was also particular. In fact, most of the early Commedia actors wore comic masks. It is asking a great deal of young actors to act only with their bodies, so I have never attempted a masked performance. This has not stopped me from employing moulage noses, warts, clown-white, and so on—materials mask-like in their effect.

Lighting is optional in the same sense that sets are. Obviously if you have access to a portable lighting setup, you will probably want to use it. On the other hand, most professional "portable" lights are heavy, and make unreasonable demands on the circuits you are likely to find if you tour the show. You can create a perfectly adequate lighting setup with two or three household dimmers set in a piece of plywood and used to control six or eight

150-watt household floods and spots mounted in clip-on holders. No gels are needed for these lights because most scenarios don't require elaborate lighting, and because as the lights are dimmed they give a lovely amber "sunset" feel to the playing space. Another advantage is that you can teach any budding "techie" how to wire and run them, even if you have little technical experience yourself—the wiring directions are right on the dimmer package.

Most schools are delighted to be offered a free theatrical performance. Commedia shows are so simple and adaptable that they tour with no fuss at all. Unlike a conventional theater piece, the director never gets tired of watching the show, since new jokes and bits are constantly being invented, discarded, reworked, set into new contexts. The more performances your students can give, the stronger they will become and the more individual and idiosyncratic their characters will be. The students will have learned to converse on stage and to listen for suggestions and verbal cues from one another.

As you gain experience with the Commedia, you will find yourself needing sources for scenarios. Oreglia, in his *The Commedia dell'Arte,* gives several in full. (One of them, called *The Enchanted Arcadia,* is so like the plot of Shakespeare's *The Tempest* that I have always been curious about which came first.) Duchartre gives a scenario for the first act of *Contrats Rompus.* I have been unable to find a translated collection of scenarios, however.

The next best thing is to write one yourself. After several productions, you should have no trouble with the creation of one of your own. All it takes is familiarity with the character, a clear sense of plot line and complication, and an awareness of what good student actors can do with them. Another alternative is to ask for help from students in creative writing classes. Writing your own can also solve casting problems, particularly if the male-female ratio in your group is lopsided.

The Commedia originally was not just a play but a total entertainment extravaganza for the people on the street. Thus it is perfectly legitimate, for example, to add as much music as you and your students feel is appropriate. I once did *The Enchanted Arcadia* as a musical, using familiar tunes from advertising, and words made up by students and staff. Frequently my actors arrive through the audience to the sound of singing, or recorder and drum. In addition to music, we have occasionally added entr'acte "bits" such as juggling, gymnastics, and fire-eating. Originally these bits were created to hold the street audience—to keep them from drifting away between the acts. Today they give young actors a chance to display talents which won't fit conveniently into the script.

When you have completed a Commedia dell' Arte performance or a tour, you may wonder where to go from there. How will the actors use their training? There are several related types of theater which can extend your students' horizons. One is Story Theatre, developed by Paul Sills, which uses many of the same kinds of techniques. Or you can go back to Moliere and try some of his bittersweet comedy with your students. (You will find a large number of familiar characters in his work, because he was a great fan of the Commedia.) Fundamentally, any piece of theater which demands interaction between character and character, and between character and audience, will be better with actors who are skilled in the Commedia dell' Arte.

Shakespeare for the Fun of It

by Libby Colman

Shakespeare is one of the world's greatest dramatists and poets of the English language. His works are little used in our schools, though they're becoming more available in the world around us.

No one questions the universality of Shakespeare's plots or characterizations. Presumably it is his locations and language which cause problems for children's response.

Last summer I watched my six-year-old respond with enthusiasm to a production of Shakespeare's *Twelfth Night*. Perhaps I had facilitated her response by a brief introduction to the play beforehand. Could I create a similar reaction in other children?

I turned to the North Bay School in Sausalito, California. It is a nongraded, open, and creative private elementary school with a socioeconomically mixed group of students. Tom Justice, director of the school, thought it would be good to introduce Shakespeare into the curriculum.

I began with my idea—to create the assumption that it is a privilege and pleasure to read Shakespeare. I started with a circle-play presentation (a whole-school assembly of children ranging from four to twelve years old) and a copy of my story-synopsis of *The Tempest*. The only other props I took were name tags—large and easy to read, one for each character. I told the students I was going to read a story written by William Shakespeare, a man who had lived 400 years ago, when people in Europe were just starting to discover the New World and didn't know much about the kinds of people who lived there.

Then I asked for a volunteer for each character, students who would act out the story while I read. After describing each character many volunteers wanted to be lords and to carry swords. Few wanted to be the prince who had to fall in love. Each volunteer put on a name tag. Everyone left over became a passenger on a ship, watching the action from a calm bay somewhere on the other side of the island.

The performance took about a half hour and went in wonderful, unexpected directions. Prospero's rotten boat was a large plastic waste-basket in which he stood, holding a tiny six-year-old in his arms. Excited confusion reigned in the shipwreck scene, but it didn't last long. Everyone wanted to see Ferdinand fall in love with Miranda so they could laugh.

The assembly accomplished more than I had expected. It created an atmosphere in which the entire school knew about Shakespeare and *The Tempest*.

The next week I got down to serious business with "big kids." We read *The Tempest* aloud, taking turns. I explained things they did not understand. Footnotes helped. The rest of the school was curious about what we were doing. I suspect that more than once, as an eleven-year-old struggled with a passage, his younger brother's interest kept him going.

To liven the activity and to tune the students into the archetypal level of the play's action, we did improvisations in the classroom. The space was cramped but the presence of "things" facilitated action. Books became logs, a desk became a pen—the actors looked for props as the need arose. Improvisations were not done each time we met. Much depended upon whether we'd read enough and if a scene was interesting.

My next step was to meet with all of the students who weren't in this class. I reread my story to them, without acting it out. Then I invited them to illustrate the story—a picture of anything that had interested them while they were listening. I'd expected to have a discussion about what they'd draw before sending them off to their tables, but each already had an idea in mind and needed no extra prompting. Many drew the character they had played in the assembly.

Under the supervision of the arts and crafts instructor, the children put together their illustrations with the text. Next they produced an original book.

I wanted to do a play of *The Tempest* after we had finished reading it, one in which their words, not too casual, are used so everyone could understand it but still have the feeling they were actually listening to Shakespeare and not a group of children. So logically the next step was to hold auditions for an all-school production. Mimeographed speeches for each character were distributed. Students from any age group could and did read for any part. Ultimately parts were assigned. The actors ranged in age from seven to twelve. We didn't have a stage and we didn't have any technical skills for lights, props, and so on. But we did have a lot of enthusiasm, a certain feeling for the play, a desire to do a good job, and an arts and crafts teacher who helped us make simple smocks, color coordinated to indicate the level of plot from which the character comes (blue for the lords, green for the characters on the island, brown for the comic characters). Most important, I had adapted the play, often paraphrasing the original speeches to shorten them making them easier for the action and understanding. I particularly tried to keep the imagery, making it a prose play.

The project "Shakespeare for the fun of it" has had many specific educational advantages. Many of the children will have had help with their reading skills, had exposure to Shakespearean language, learned certain technical things about poetry and drama, practiced moving in front of an audience, and had involvement in specific arts and crafts projects.

Most important of all, the children learned that Shakespeare is exciting and fun. Someday in the future, if they hear of a production of *The Tempest,* hopefully they will try to get to see it. And when they do, most of them will understand the action and be able to follow most of the dialogue.

Readers Theatre by Children

by Patrick Groff

Readers Theatre, as it is usually practiced, is a dramatic procedure in which the roles in a play are read by individual performers with little of the staging that normally accompanies conventional theatre. Rather than memorizing dialogue, the performers in Readers Theatre read from hand-carried scripts. The readers sit or stand and use their voices, rather than action, to focus their attention (and that of any audience) on the ideas in the literature. Facial expressions and body movements are restricted and suggestive. This brief description of Readers Theatre indicates how plain and uncomplicated this activity seems in comparison with conventional theatre practices. As Coger and White reflect, ''The keynote in staging Readers Theatre is simplicity'' (1: 87).

THE PRESENT STATUS OF READERS THEATRE

Readers Theatre has been described as ''a great motivational device for children'' (2: 171), an especially valuable means of stirring children's interest in literature, developing their insight, self-confidence, and academic skills (3: 3). Readers Theatre is seldom recommended as a technique to use with children, however. Perhaps authorities on elementary-school English know too little about this way of interpreting literature to recommend it. As the technique becomes better known, it may be more widely used.

The oral interpretation of literature—choral reading, choral recitation—is an ancient art. Still, Readers Theatre is often described as ''a most interesting new development'' or invention (4: 263). Grimes and Mattingly (5) trace the use of what is now called Readers Theatre back to 1806. The current heightened interest in Readers Theatre may stem from the productions of ''Don Juan in Hell'' by the company of Charles Laughton, Agnes Moorehead, Sir Cedric Hardwicke and Charles Boyer in 1951. Since then the technique has grown in popularity. In 1972 Bennett wrote: ''Perhaps one-fifth of all theatrical productions at large American universities are done as Readers Theatre'' (6: 8). Even as late as 1966, however, Readers Theatre was still being called ''experimental group reading,'' a form of multiple reading ''still in experimental stages'' (7: 290).

Readers Theatre has not been widely recommended for children most likely because it is, in truth, a formal dramatic experience. In Readers Theatre children are expected to practice the parts they will read. Their readings are required to be faithful to the wording and the intentions of the authors of the scripts. The aversion that experts in elementary-school language arts have for formal drama may well account for their lack of enthusiasm for Readers Theatre.

Before the advent of the term ''Readers Theatre'' in 1945 (1), some elementary-school teachers doubtless conducted activities similar to Readers Theatre, and some teachers have done so since then. Over the years imaginative teachers have involved children in activities know as multiple reading, concert reading, group reading, dramatic reading, library play-reading, and interpretative reading. Teachers who have used variations of Readers Theatre with children have been enthusiastic about its values. Why? The question can be answered by describing the major elements of Readers Theatre and some standards for conducting it. The description may encourage teachers who are unfamiliar with Readers Theatre to try it.

As late as 1963 there were ''many arguments regarding the form a particular presentation [of Readers Theatre] should take'' (8: 159). Some contend that ''there is no 'one way' to do Readers Theatre'' (9: 334), that ''no hard-and-fast ground rules apply'' for Readers Theatre with children (10: 169). Nonetheless, there are some standard procedures that elementary-school teachers who are introducing Readers Theatre use and some orthodox assumptions that teachers should make about it.

THE READER

Foremost is the role of the readers. Each reader who is assigned or who chooses a role in this activity must take the responsibility of studying the part carefully. Readers must consider the theme, the mood or the tone, the imagery, the action, and the climax of the play. The job of the child reader is to search ''for the nuances of meaning behind each line'' (2: 170). In studying a part each reader becomes aware not only of his role but also of the roles of the other readers. The goal of each reader in Readers Theatre is "to clarify, illuminate, extend, or provide insights into the particular literary text being presented" (11: 3). Thus each child "tries to project an invisible scene or scenes into the listeners' imaginations" (6: 10). The readers try to attain this goal by use of the voice—through voice quality, volume, rate of delivery, pitch, and intonation: gestures and movement are merely suggestive or kept to a minimum.

Some experts on Readers Theatre argue that "any definition of Readers Theatre that relies on the physical presence of the manuscript (or any other conventional device) to establish the medium rests on a monumental misconception of artistic form" (12: 65). In Readers Theatre by children, however, it is essential that each reader have a script. Because one major purpose of Readers Theatre is to strengthen children's oral reading abilities, children are asked to read aloud rather than to memorize their parts. This stipulation is appropriate because it is less difficult and less time consuming to read a script aloud than to memorize it. The physical presence of the script is a psychological comfort for children, reducing any anxiety they may have about forgetting their lines or about not knowing when to speak. Organized in this way, Readers Theatre is likely to be less threatening or demanding for children than involvement in conventional children's theatre.

THE NARRATOR

Readers Theatre uses narrators. The child who takes the role of narrator may volunteer for it or he may be chosen. It is important that the role of the narrator be a minor one. The activities of the readers are more interesting to the audience than the words of the narrator. Still, the narrator is necessary. First of all, the narrator introduces the activity, using a story-telling manner. Beyond that purpose, the narrator is necessary to describe essential aspects of the material not covered by the dialogue and to relate the physical action of the play, because in Readers Theatre physical movement is restricted. The narrator makes clear any complicated twist in the plot, sets scenes, introduces characters, or interprets or reflects on anything otherwise impossible to include in the dialogue. The narrator speaks as if what is being said is not intended for the readers to hear. The implication is that the readers already know what the narrator is saying. Preferably, plays used in Readers Theatre by children do not have characters who say only a few lines. The script is so prepared that each reader has about the same number of lines. If a play has minor characters, their few lines can be rewritten into narration and read by the narrator.

When the script in Readers Theatre is adapted from a story the narrator reads passages in the adaptation that reveal the characters' thoughts. The narrator would read the italicized part of the following line: " 'What did they live on?' *said Alice, who always took a great interest in questions of eating and drinking.*" In the line, " 'They couldn't have done that, you know,' *Alice gently remarked,*" the narrator would not read the italicized portion. The audience could interpret what is indicated by the reader's tone of voice.

STAGING

The staging of Readers Theatre further distinguishes it from conventional drama. In Readers Theatre the reader usually sits on a chair or a stool, holding a script. The use of lecterns, or other stands on which scripts are rested, is discouraged. They tend to pose barriers between the readers and their audience, and act to unduly restrict any dramatic movements a reader may wish to make. Maclay advises that "there is not much value in using them" (11: 54). In Readers Theatre the readers normally sit because there is no pretense of giving a play. Thus only a limited amount of stage technique is used. Some experts in Readers Theatre insist that the reader keep his eyes on the script and remain as motionless as possible (3: 334). This restriction on children in Readers Theatre is inappropriate. Bacon writes: "Nothing is worse than a reading in which the readers simply look into their manuscripts without reference to the audience" (13: 415). In any event, because of children's proclivity for activity it is advisable that they be allowed to indulge in some stage movements when reading.

The issue of stage movements raises the question of entrances and exits into and out of scenes. The problem is almost always present, but it can be reduced by keeping the number of readers in the cast as small as possible. In Readers Theatre children can step forward or stand when "entering" scenes. (Standing is also used to emphasize a certain point in the play.) Children can turn their backs to the audience when "exiting" a scene. Even though Bacon describes the precedure as a "questionable practice" (13: 414), it seems to work well with children. To indicate exits and entrances, children can simply raise and lower their heads, although this device may cause undue strain. Spotlights can be used to distinguish the readers in a scene. Some experts say, "Perhaps the most unobtrusive and effective guidepost to stepping into or out of the picture [in Readers Theatre] is simply that of opening and closing the manuscript" (14: 395). Of all the means of effecting entrances and exits this seems the least desirable for children, for it poses the possibility of losing one's place in the script and creating a hazard to the flow of the production.

On the seating arrangement in Readers Theatre, the audience must clearly see the face of each reader. The requirement is critical. Once that requirement has been met, the teacher of Readers Theatre may want to consider the psychological effects of the placement of readers. They may be placed at different levels to indicate prominence or level of authority. They may be arranged into groups to suggest that groups are opposed to, or in union with, one another. The teacher of Readers Theatre must work out these and other similar problems for each individual play, keeping in mind its organization and theme.

Experts in Readers Theatre agree on seating arrangements in this activity but do not agree on another issue—whether readers in Readers Theatre should turn their heads or their bodies to address one another when reading. This is called ''onstage focus.'' Some argue that an onstage focus violates the essence of Readers Theatre which, they say, demands that the reader always focus his or her attention ''offstage,'' or out to the audience. Lee (9) maintains that the reader should never turn to look at the person whose speech he is answering. Bacon disagrees. He believes that readers ''may look at one another from time to time to make their conversing seem natural'' (13: 410). Sessions and Holland agree that ''it makes no vital difference whether the readers face the audience or their fellow players'' (4: 264). In Readers Theatre an onstage focus seems much more natural for children, and therefore its use should not be discouraged. For children, ''It seems far more natural for readers to be actively interplaying with each other than to try to place an artificial barrier between themselves'' (4: 264). It is doubtful that an onstage focus detracts from the audience's role or involvement. Dalan (15) found that for adult audiences of Readers Theatre the change of focus from offstage to onstage did not significantly affect comprehension of the literature that was being read. It is unlikely, then, that child audiences will suffer if an onstage focus is used in Readers Theatre.

VISUAL AND AUDITORY AIDS

Should visual and auditory aids be used in Readers Theatre? Does Readers Theatre require scenery, lighting, props, makeup, and costumes? In general, such aspects of conventional theatre are ''seldom, if ever, needed'' (5: 336). As noted earlier, the readers in Readers Theatre are expected to use their voices to project the mental and the emotional complexities of the characters being interpreted: the readers are not ex-pected to act like or look like a character being portrayed. Readers Theatre aims to make sure that its appeal is not primarily visual. If scenery, props, costumes, and makeup are used they should be suggestive, not literal, as in conventional theatre. This does not mean that lighting is not useful. Black-outs are an effective way to signal the end of a scene and thus may become the means for readers to get into and out of a scene. As already noted, some Readers Theatre spotlights readers who are in a scene. The background or setting for a scene in Readers Theatre can be effectively established by use of a slide projector.

The teacher of Readers Theatre is often encouraged to experiment with visual and auditory aids as interest and time allow. Music and sound effects create mood and evoke emotion in Readers Theatre. Teachers of Readers Theatre have found that children enjoy constructing costumes and scenery that suggest who the characters in a play are and what the setting is. Props are seldom used in Readers Theatre by children, however. The scripts that children read are hand-held and restrict the use of props. Makeup is rarely used in Readers Theatre by children. Applying and removing makeup are not skills most teachers understand well. If the Readers Theatre production is given in school the time needed for management of makeup is usually too demanding.

THE MATERIALS

Plays are the dominant materials used in Readers Theatre, but other kinds of literature, even nonfiction, have been found to be compatible with this form of oral interpretation. Certain guidelines should govern the choice of material, whatever it may be—plays especially written for children such as those found in basal readers, plays in literary anthologies, plays in collections designed for children's use (16, 17, 18), or adaptations of stories or nonfiction. As already suggested, any material that depends heavily on extensive stage business, or movement, or scenery should be avoided. Generally speaking, written content that is reflective, highly descriptive, or abstract is not good for Readers Theatre with this age group. One writer disagrees with this advice. Geeting writes: "Plays which lack plot and may be slow when acted often lend themselves beautifully to group interpretation" (7: 290-91). It may be wiser, though, to use material that has a logical plot and actions that the readers and their audience can easily interpret. The material should have felicity of style and well-defined compelling characters who speak a moving dialogue. Thes best scripts exemplify authentic, familiar, even humorous drama. The climax should be satisfyingly resolute: the play should not dissolve into a discordant closure. Beyond this, it is proper to adapt short, rather than extended pieces of material, especially when the children involved are unaccustomed to performing in Readers Theatre.

Almost all literature used in Readers Theatre, including plays, must be adapted to some extent. For plays, adaptation often means assigning to the narrator anything that is not directly expressed in the dialogue. Because there is little dramatic movement in Readers Theatre the narrator must tell the audience what the actor's movements in conventional theatre would otherwise reveal. The adaptation of nonplay material for Readers Theatre requires several other kinds of preparation. At first, the teacher may well do any rewriting that is necessary. Later, children who have shown that they can master this kind of composition can take on the rewriting. The rewriters should be faithful to the author, keeping as much of the original wording as possible. At the same time it is usually necessary for the rewriter to eliminate unneeded scenes especially to create short scripts for Readers Theatre. The narrator in Readers Theatre can summarize some of the scenes that are omitted, and some narrative in the original can be changed to dialogue. After such abridgments it is often necessary to write carefully constructed links from each new scene to the next one to retain continuity. Changes in the original material are sometimes needed to help the readers and the audience understand. Short sentences and simple vocabulary often help.

Good examples of how stories for children have been changed to plays for Readers Theatre are found in Coger and White's book (1) and in McCaslin's (10). Their adaptations suggest that this process is not so difficult as it is time consuming. Wise teachers will instruct their pupils on how to do this writing. Children can rewrite successfully from media other than print. I recently viewed the performance of an effective rewrite for Readers Theatre of the television program, "Welcome Back, Kotter." The rewriter was a middle-grade pupil.

THE DIRECTOR

In the initial stages of Readers Theatre by children the teacher will take the role of director. Gradually pupils can assume the duties of organizing and directing Readers Theatre as well as selecting and adapting materials. Children have not only performed notable Readers Theatre but have made remarkable choices of script and displayed distinguished skills in directing. To fulfill the responsibilities of a director, children need to know the general meaning of the script. For this purpose it is appropriate to have them paraphrase the content. Children need help in understanding the attitudes and the motives of the characters they will orally interpret. To assist with this interpretation, the director might have the reader ask, "Why does my character say *what* he does *when* he does?" Any other means the director can use to achieve a critical reading of the script should be employed.

The director can help readers in other ways. Stage fright is sometimes a problem. It can be overcome by concentrating on the text and forgetting about oneself. Readers should be led to do the best they can, convinced that their efforts will be well received. They should be encouraged to show enthusiastic, honest, and open emotions in their performances. The director might say, "Don't block your feelings. Let them show." In Readers Theatre it is better to demonstrate too much emotion than too little, for it is easy to restrain excessive amounts of sentiment.

The director must teach readers and narrators to speak clearly and loudly. Most children especially need to be told to speak louder. To improve children's enunciation and articulation they should be asked to emphasize the verbs in their lines. Words to be stressed can be marked with different colors to signal changes in the mood or the emotion of the speaker. A red line can be used as a signal for loudness or greater emotion, a blue line for a more subdued tone, and so on. Readings of individual children can be tape recorded, and the director can critique their delivery. Readers and narrators in Readers Theatre must be taught to take extra time to speak more slowly than they usually do. The director might demonstrate. Speaking at a measured pace, he or she can give each syllable in a word a deliberate emphasis and clearly articulate the final sounds in words.

The director should remind children of the facial expressions and hand gestures they know and use in daily life to express fear, pleading, accusations, reassurance, humor, threat, negative feelings, and other emotions. These gestures and expressions are practiced best with examples from lines in a script.

As soon as possible, the director should aim to have the entire class "work concurrently and experimentally within the confines of the ordinary classroom," as Logan, Logan, and Paterson say (19: 438). These writers advise that a class of normal size "can be readily divided into seven working groups, each member actively engaged in the reading-interpreting assignment" (19: 438). Engaging the entire class is no short-term goal, however. It requires adroit management on the part of the director. If the pitfalls of total group participation in oral interpretation, as described by Barnfield (20), are to be avoided, it is best to move slowly into the involvement of all children in a class in Readers Theatre at the same time.

The director in Readers Theatre might start by instructing a group of easily managed pupils (not necessarily the best readers in the class). Then, as other children in the class become intrigued by the performances of the initial party, new companies can be formed. At this point children from the original group that has performed Readers Theatre can act as directors or assistant directors for newly formed groups of children. To conduct more than one circle of performers at the same time poses the problem of the overlap of voices and the confusion that ensues. The director may find it necessary to enlist teacher's aides, parents, or other volunteers to supervise rehearsals of separate groups of children in Readers Theatre as groups move into school hallways or assembly or conference rooms. Readers Theatre can be practiced outside the regular school hours—during lunch periods and after school.

The director of Readers Theatre, in assigning or recruiting volunteers for roles, should consider any child who can read aloud a potential participant. At levels higher than the elementary school the best readers available are usually given the most prestigious or dominant roles in a Readers Theatre production. This is not appropriate with Readers Theatre for children. For children, "the primary values [of Readers Theatre] are derived from the selection and interpretation of the material and the practice in reading aloud" (10: 163). The important parts of a script can be read by children who need the personality-enhancing stimulants of Readers Theatre. In short, Readers Theatre for children, as opposed to Readers Theatre in general, is more concerned with the processes of this activity and their effects on individual children than with a finished product.

This attitude toward Readers Theatre does not prohibit performances by children, on occasion, outside their classroom. As children grow more proficient in this aspect of formal theatrics they will want to perform for outsiders. Out-of-class performance is never the primary reason for conducting Readers Theatre with children, however.

Rehearsal in Readers Theatre for children has a different meaning than it ordinarily has because the process, not the completed product, is of the greatest consideration. Rehearsal is chiefly a time for trying out different children in various roles in Readers Theatre as an experimental encounter for readers. Because the results of this encounter are not always predictable, the director of Readers Theatre by children usually does not demand predetermined levels of performance from each child who takes part.

CONCLUSIONS

Teachers who have used Readers Theatre with children affirm that "though difficult and challenging, Readers Theatre is an effective and satisfying technique" (9: 335). It develops the child's insight into and interest in literature, along with oral and critical reading skills. Readers Theatre provides an easy outlet for communal performance by the shy child. Beyond this, it affords children experiences with formal drama and therefore with a taste of the theatre. It uses children's creative impulses and helps teach them cooperation and self-confidence. Teachers have reported that Readers Theatre takes less of their personal attention to accomplish than either conventional drama or creative drama. It functions well, then, as a prerequisite for both these dramatic forms.

Readers Theatre by children has received little attention from experts in elementary-school English, but there is no reason why teachers interested in introducing some aspects of formal drama into the language arts curriculum should not use Readers Theatre for this purpose. Teachers who need or desire an intriguing new approach to language and literature may find this pathway through Readers Theatre.

NOTES

1. Irene Leslie Coger and Melvin R. White. *Readers Theatre Handbook: A Dramatic Approach to Literature*. Glenview, Illinois: Scott, Foresman, 1973.

2. John F. Savage. *Effective Communication: Language Arts Instruction in the Elementary School*. Chicago, Illinois: Science Research Associates, 1977.

3. Iz Crain and William Franklin Smith. "Readers Theatre Reaches the Young," *Readers Theatre News, 4* (Fall, 1976), 3–4.

4. Virgil D. Sessions and Jack B. Holland. *Your Role in Oral Interpretation*. Boston, Massachusetts: Holbrook, 1968.

5. Wilma H. Grimes and Alethea Smith Mattingly. *Interpretation: Writer, Reader, Audience*. San Francisco, California: Wadsworth, 1961.

6. Gordon C. Bennett. *Readers Theatre Comes to Church*. Richmond, Virginia: John Knox, 1972.

7. Baxter M. Geeting. *Interpretation for Our Time*. Dubuque, Iowa: Wm. C. Brown, 1966.

8. Irene Leslie Coger. "Interpreter's Theatre: Theatre of the Mind," *Quarterly Journal of Speech, 49* (April, 1963), 157–64.

9. Charlotte I. Lee. *Oral Interpretation*. Boston, Massachusetts: Houghton Mifflin, 1965.

10. Nellie McCaslin. *Creative Dramatics in the Classroom*. New York, New York: David McKay, 1974.

11. Joanna Hawkins Maclay. *Readers Theatre: Toward a Grammar of Practice*. New York, New York: Random House, 1971.

12. Jere Veilleux. "Some Aphorisms for Readers Theatre," *Speech Teacher, 21* (January, 1972), 64–66.

13. Wallace A. Bacon. *The Art of Interpretation*. New York, New York: Holt, Rinehart and Winston, 1972.

14. Keith Brooks, Eugene Bahn, and L. La Mont Okey. *The Communicative Act of Oral Interpretation*. Boston, Massachusetts: Allyn and Bacon, 1975.

15. Nonna Childress Dalan. "Audience Response to Use of Offstage Focus and Onstage Focus in Readers Theatre," *Speech Monographs, 38* (March, 1971), 74–77.

16. Donald D. Durrell and Alice B. Crossley. *Favorite Plays for Classroom Reading*. Boston, Massachusetts: Plays, Inc., 1965.

17. Donald D. Durrell and Alice B. Crossley. *Thirty Plays for Classroom Reading*. Boston, Massachusetts: Plays, Inc., 1968 (Also see the magazine, *Plays.*)

18. Paul Nolan. *Round-the-World Plays for Young People*. Boston, Massachusetts: Plays, Inc., 1961.

19. Lillian M. Logan, Virgil G. Logan, and Leona Paterson. *Creative Communication: Teaching the Language Arts*. Toronto, Canada: McGraw-Hill Ryerson, 1972.

20. Gabriel Barnfield. *Creative Drama in Schools*. New York, New York: Hart, 1968.

PART IV
Social Studies and
Values Clarification

Introductory Comments

Social studies usually includes the study of home and family, foreign lands, and our own history. Because values clarification can be included as a part of the study of human culture, it has been placed in this section.

"Drama is gaining increasing importance in the social studies curriculum because it helps students focus their attention on a historical event, understand human motivations and feelings and better retain key facts and basic concepts" states Edward Berry in "Dramatic Steps into History." Berry further illuminates these ideas and describes his approach for relating the past to contemporary times.

Dennis L. Allen and Robert J. Corey actually portray historical characters, and the article "Will the Mystery Guests Please Sign In?" relates their experiences while posing as famous people "in character, in costume, and in person." Katherine B. Murphy, in "On the Trail of Lewis and Clark," explores social studies through simulation drama about explorers. Her "treks through time" could serve as a model for many imagined adventures, and her practical advice provides an easy plan to follow.

Peer interaction, when coupled with dramatization, can, according to Gloria Jane Wallin, be a method to provide a stimulus for growth in moral judgment and contribute to a child's development. Her article, "Fostering Moral Development through Creative Dramatics," describes 3 dramatizations based upon situations through which children learn to make moral decisions.

Violet Asmuth examines the teacher's role in teaching values. "Two Hits with One Throw: Drama and Values" shows how dramatization can help to achieve the goal of developing rational processes and value judgment.

Dramatic Steps into History

by Edward Berry

"It was a catastrophe!" This was one teacher's comment on her efforts to help students dramatize the signing of the Declaration of Independence.

"Five students were seated around a table to portray the signers. They just sat and giggled for two minutes. Finally, one of the kids said, 'What are we supposed to do?' Fortunately, while I was trying to think of an answer, the bell rang for recess."

Drama is gaining increasing importance in the social studies curriculum, because it helps students focus their attention on an historical event, understand human motivations and feelings and better retain key facts and basic concepts. This teacher, like so many others, recognizes the value of drama but does not know exactly *how* to proceed.

I have developed an approach that takes the uncertainty out of using classroom drama and provides a simple framework of five sequential steps: identify the event, explore the characters, create original background scenes, combine the scenes into a story connected with the event, relate the event to contemporary times. Youngsters of almost any age or ability group can follow the steps successfully with some guidance from you.

FLASHBACK

One of my first experiences with social studies drama provides a "before" and "after" picture that will give you a general idea of how these steps function. I was working with a fourth-grade class in Caroline Brevard Elementary School, Tallahassee, Fla., that was studying how the Pilgrims governed themselves. I wanted the children to understand the basic concept of representative government.

In a short improvisation they were to pretend they were Pilgrims, nominate several members of the colony (class) who felt best qualified to represent them, give several nominating speeches and hold an election. Then I planned to have them make comparisons between the Pilgrims' democracy and their student council.

To my dismay, the entire activity lasted only 10 minutes, and the students had not grasped the basic concept. After thinking about how I could solve this problem, I decided to try the five-step approach.

The next time I met with the class, I divided the students into small groups. I asked each one to think of one reason why the Pilgrims needed to elect representatives, plan a short scene illustrating the reason and act it out for the other students. To the students' and my amazement, they depicted a variety of logical reasons. One group showed how difficult it was to assemble the entire colony from the fields. Another depicted a lengthy meeting that lasted three days in order to hear every person's opinion. A third dramatized an emergency that could not be handled by the colonies because there was no provision for such situations.

After combining some of the scenes into a logical story, the students again enacted the election of representatives. This time every student could see the necessity for representative democracy and could draw more accurate comparisons with their student council.

To understand the specifics involved in each step, suppose that you and your students are studying the white settlement of the Indiana Territory in the beginning of the nineteenth century. The situation involved the Shawnee chief Tecumseh, leader of a confederacy of Native American tribes, and William Henry Harrison, governor of the territory.

Harrison signed treaties with individual chiefs in the area to obtain land for white settlement. Tecumseh contended that these agreements were not valid unless all the tribes in the confederacy agreed. This conflict led to the Battle of Tippecanoe that resulted in Tecumseh's defeat and the confederacy's dissolution.

IDENTIFY THE EVENT

Establishing a purpose and preparing students are the focus of the first step. It's important that you ask yourself what basic concept you want your students to understand from the dramatization of the specific event. In this example, it might be that groups of people view the same issue differently.

Then make sure that the students know the basic facts by reading a textbook, biographies or other books, doing some research in the library and using audiovisual materials. After they have some familiarity with the event, open a discussion and ask the children what they think the key ideas are. They might point to the Native Americans' dissatisfaction with their treaties or the settlers' desire to establish their homesteads as quickly as possible. At this point you can explain the basic concept you want them to learn and talk about how the key ideas the children suggested are related to that concept.

Conclude this step by having several children act out an incident in the event, such as the battle between Tecumseh's tribes and Harrison's soldiers. You may find that the enactment is superficial and quick. Don't worry. This is simply a tryout to make sure that everyone understands the incident.

CHARACTER EXPLORATION

In the second step, the children explore the personalities, appearances and opinions of the characters they portray. Ask the students to name all the participants in the event, including main characters and groups, and write them on the board. In this example, the characters would be Tecumseh and Harrison, the Native Americans, the settlers and perhaps the soldiers.

Next define for the student what the term *in character* means—moving, talking and thinking exactly as the character would. For our purposes, *character* means the men and women who were part of the event. Explain that in the following activity you will be observing how well they can act in character.

For each name listed on the board, have the students describe how they think the character would think, look, move. Students might say that Harrison dislikes Native Americans, that he is a straight-backed, commanding, no-nonsense figure or that he's a man in the middle trying to mediate the demands of both sides. Volunteers then pantomime the character doing some logical activity based on the suggestions. Repeat the pantomiming activity for each character.

For this activity students are to pretend that the character is alone and ignore classmates. Since the pantomimists do not interact with each other and it's not necessary to have an audience, each child in the classroom can join in this imaginary exercise. Avoid calling attention to students who are having difficulty pantomiming or acting out their roles. Instead, positively reinforce those who are doing well.

Now students are ready to add speech to their characterizations. Divide the class into pairs and have each pair portray two characters exchanging their views on the event. If the pairs represent two opposing characters, you may find that they resort to verbal fighting. To avoid this, point out that the two people must find logical reasons to disagree with each other. Then have these partners reverse roles. Repeat the activity for the other characters.

Tecumseh and Harrison might have this exchange: Tecumseh could say that the settlers were infringing on the Native Americans' land. Harrison might respond that they agreed to this by treaty.

ORIGINAL BACKGROUND SCENES

The third step involves creating scenes that show why the people in the event feel as they do. These scenes must be based closely on the facts of the event.

Divide the class into groups of four or five, each group representing one side in the event. After using five or 10 minutes for scene planning, each group will act out its own imaginary but logical scene showing that side's viewpoint.

Suppose a group represents the Native Americans. These students might depict empty-handed hunters telling the tribe that there's no meat because white settlers had frightened away the deer.

You may find that the groups argue over whose idea to use, or you may hear frequent complaints about not having enough time. In this case, tell the students to go ahead with one of the first ideas they come up with and spend the remainder of their time planning the details.

If you feel it's necessary, emphasize the importance of being a courteous audience. The best approach is to remind students that *they* will want an attentive audience. This is also the time to get some critical discussion going with the students on whether or not each scene could really have happened and the reasons why. When the scenes for one side are finished, divide the class into different groups and repeat the activity for the other side.

THE WHOLE STORY

In the fourth step, students create a story that culminates in the basic incident (in this case, the war between Tecumseh's and Harrison's forces). Ask the children to choose two or three scenes from each side's viewpoint from step three. Discuss the order of the scenes. If the sequence seems unclear, simply alternate scenes of both sides, but be sure to place the basic incident at the end. Briefly list each scene on the board in the order of presentation.

Choose several students to act out the entire story. Then discuss the results with them. You might want to pose these questions: Did the actors accurately portray the characters? What could be done to improve the story? What have you learned about the event in relation to the basic concept?

Have members of the audience and actors switch places and play out the story again. If changes occur in the action, discuss why. To provide more insight into the event, your students may want to create other stories in a similar manner.

CONTEMPORARY TIMES

A broad understanding of the basic concept also involves being able to compare and apply it to a different situation. This is the final step.

Ask the children to think about and discuss a relatively current situation that might be similar to the one they have just portrayed. It could be an international, national, local or school incident. For example, the recent Wounded Knee episode in South Dakota reflects several of the same frustrations between Native Americans and the government that existed in 1811. If students are unable to come up with a current event to compare, suggest one to them and explain the background. Or, they could research the facts themselves in the public library.

As in step three, divide the class into groups and ask each one to create an imaginary scene from the event, such as the meeting at which the American Indian Movement decided to take over Wounded Knee to call attention to its position. Then, the children can use the same process as in step four to build a story composed of the scenes and end with a possible outcome, such as the protesters agreeing to leave Wounded Knee peacefully. Instead of simply repeating history, discuss other ways that the problem might have been resolved.

Using this approach effectively requires only a little practice and experimentation. Whatever the historical time and place your students encounter, social studies drama can provide an important ''you are there'' dimension.

Will the Mystery Guests Please Sign In?

by Dennis L. Allen and Robert J. Corey

"Mary had a little lamb.
Its fleece was white as snow.
And everywhere that Mary went.
The lamb was sure to go."

In our classrooms, Thomas A. Edison recites this verse via a record. Standing nearby is the "real" Edison—a man in shirt-sleeves with arm garters, a celluloid collar and tousled gray hair. As our students listen to this voice from the past and look at the costumed figure, they make a memorable connection between the inventor and his invention—the phonograph player.

Real people make history. Conveying this idea to children, as many teachers know, isn't always easy. Pictures and print can only supply two-dimensional details on a historical figure's appearance, life-style and impact on events. But showing youngsters the flesh-and-blood reality of famous people in character, in costume and in person gives an additional perspective. We have found that portraying American historical personalities through monthly mystery events can be very successful.

During our classroom visits, we talk to the children about "our" accomplishments, relate personal anecdotes and use films, records or tapes that depict events the historical figures were involved in. By enriching our social studies curriculum in this way, we help the children gain a more solid understanding of U.S. history. But, most important, they can see for themselves the human motivations, interests and feelings of these very real history-makers.

THE GUEST LIST

When we first discussed the idea of presenting mystery events, we decided to set up some criteria for selecting the historical personalities. We finally concluded that the characters would come from 10 representative time periods of American history to correspond to the 10 months of the school year, represent a variety of professions and be easily recognized and remembered by the children.

As a result our ''guest list'' includes such notables as Ben Franklin and Paul Revere, Lewis and Clark, Ulysses S. Grant and Robert E. Lee, Mark Twain and Tom Sawyer, the Wright brothers, Thomas A. Edison and Henry Ford, Laurel and Hardy and ''Buzz'' Aldrin, Neil Armstrong and Michael Collins. We worked as a team on our project to portray two related figures for each event, but you could impersonate one man or woman to represent a historical era. Other characters you may want to consider are Betsy Ross, Molly Pitcher, Clara Barton, Susan B. Anthony, Harriet Tubman, George Washington Carver, Jim Thorpe, Martin Luther King, Jesse Owens and Cesar Chavez.

Once our program was sketched out, we approached Principal David Pumpa for support and feedback. He provided us with a flexible schedule on our mystery event days, which allowed us to visit other schools, as well as other classrooms in our own school. We also received assistance from our elementary supervisor, Wallace Murray, who volunteered to be Abraham Lincoln when we appeared as Lee and Grant and ''Buzz'' Aldrin when we impersonated the astronauts.

PREPARING THE SCENARIO

It takes about a month to plan and prepare for each event. First, we meet several times to discuss the content of each character presentation. Using a variety of references, such as biographies and encyclopedias, we take notes on the major events in a character's life and the political, social and economic circumstances of the time. When all our background notes are complete, we decide who will represent which character. We put our notes in speech form, altering the vocabulary and detail somewhat to suit our two different audiences—primary and intermediate graders. Then we go over the notes until we have a polished performance. For example, when ''U.S. Grant'' made his presentation, he gave an overall view of life during and after the Civil War, describing his war experiences and his years in the White House.

Whenever we can we try to relate human interest stories that illuminate the character's personality. Grant told the children how he acquired the initials "U.S." When he first enrolled at West Point, he discovered that his sponsor had mistakenly reported his name as Ulysses Simpson Grant, instead of his christened name, Hiram Ulysses Grant. Thereafter, his classmates called him "U.S." and "Uncle Sam." Grant had often been teased as a child for the initials H.U.G., so he readily adopted his new name. Later on, the letters came to stand for "unconditional surrender."

Childhood experiences really grab the children's attention, especially the younger students. Such stories not only add a personal touch but also help the students realize that history-makers were once their age. Edison related his confrontation with an ear-pulling conductor who caused his deafness, and the "Wright brothers" described how much they loved to play with toy helicopters.

WARDROBE WORK

The next step involves searching out the items we need to make our costumes. We visited a local costume shop, army surplus store, the Salvation Army and Goodwill and asked for donations from parents and friends. For example, we fashioned Grant's and Lee's beards from a braid of stage hair. Lee's gray coat and pants came from a Salvation Army store. Grant's "dress blues" materialized from a truck driver's jacket and a pair of navy pants. Six star-shaped buttons completed the ensemble.

Our search for realistic costumes left no stone unturned. An unlikely source, a local motorcycle dealer, provided us with a perfect wardrobe to portray the astronauts—silver all-weather suits and "space" helmets.

STAGE PROPS

The third step in our planning sessions involves collecting pertinent audiovisual materials and display items for each character. From the local public library we obtained numerous biographies on several reading levels for the children to look through after the presentation. The library was also our source for a number of inexpensive-to-rent films. We were able to find footage of the Wright brothers' historic flights. A film on Mark Twain's Hannibal, Missouri (*Mark Twain and Tom Sawyer*, International Film Bureau), included scenes of the secret cave, the whitewashed fence and the Mississippi River that all served as inspiration for his classic novel *Tom Sawyer*.

Maps, brochures, pictures, posters and information sheets came from several government agencies. We addressed our requests to the National Aeronautics and Space Administration at the Lewis Research Center, Office of Educational Services (21000 Brook Park Rd., Cleveland, OH 44135) and the U.S. Government Printing Office (710 N. Capital St., N.W., Washington, DC 20402). As part of our materials search, we visited Greenfield Village and the Henry Ford Museum, a historical park in Dearborn, Mich. There we made slides of Ford's home and workshop and took pictures of the Wright brothers' bicycle shop and Edison's Menlo Park laboratories.

During Grant's and Lee's visit, we showed two sound filmstrips from the set *The Civil War* (Society for Visual Education) that depict the generals meeting at Appomattox Court House. As the pictures of Lee's and Grant's historic meeting flashed across the screen, many of the students' eyes darted back and forth between the filmstrips and the "live" generals in front of them. We also displayed two genuine Civil War swords and biographies on the two men from the school library.

When we portrayed Laurel and Hardy to emphasize American's contribution to the world of entertainment, films became the focus of everyone's attention. With the comedians' famous expressions on our faces, we arrived in our derbies. The children watched and laughed at the pair cavorting and bumbling through *The Clown Princes of Hollywood* (Killian Shows Inc.), one of their 1930's productions. This film also compares various film techniques and describes the development of early movies.

COMING ATTRACTIONS

Preparing our audiences for an upcoming mystery event is the fourth part of our plans. A few days beforehand, we post signs that announce the date and time. To create suspense we also drop a few helpful clues about our carefully guarded secret identities. Classroom and faculty room curiosity is so strong that sometimes we are forced to take unusual measures, such as keeping the list of books we take out of the school library for research top secret!

These hints usually take the form of a duplicated bulletin that mentions the field of work the characters were involved in and the time period. The children can then do some independent research to try and find out who the characters might be. They write their guesses on slips of paper and drop them in one of the "mystery boxes" strategically placed in the hallways. The names of the students who guess correctly are announced on the public-address sytem the morning of the event, and they receive a certificate praising their study skills.

Sometimes, however, our strategy backfires. Prior to our Laurel and Hardy impersonations, we told the youngsters that they would find a clue in the television listings for a particular night. We knew one of the comedians' old movies was to be shown. What we didn't know was that a salute to Walt Whitman and a special program about various Revolutionary patriots were also televised that night. Despite the confusion, the kids enjoyed debating the pros and cons of who the character would be.

PERSONAL APPEARANCES

The last step is scheduling our personal appearances so that as many students as possible can attend our mystery event. Mr. Pumpa arranges for substitute teachers to take over our classes for the day. In the morning we visit three other local elementary schools. In the afternoon we meet with the classes in our own school—the primary grades first, then the intermediate grades.

No actor could have better audiences. The children listen to our presentations very attentively and are eager to handle the display items, leaf through the books or brochures and discuss the related historical events. For days after each event, the school librarians tell us they are flooded with requests for books on the characters. When we set up suggestion boxes, we find them stuffed with ideas for future events. Toward the end of the year, the number of students who can guess our identities correctly increases quite a bit, and we notice that many of them can accurately recall details of the characters' lives.

Some of the children even undertake their own mini-events, complete with reports and homemade costumes. In one instance, ''General Custer'' walked away from the Battle of the Little Big Horn alive!

At 3:10 P.M. the day is finally over. We step out of the characters that we have lived with for a month and begin the process again for our next ''mystery event.'' For all of us, studying about the people who made history has become a joyful and exciting learning experience.

On the Trail of Lewis and Clark

by Katherine B. Murphy

When I was a child, playing "explorer" along the banks of creeks and streams was a popular recreation for my friends and me. Cortez, de Soto, La Salle and others were all characters in "Saturday matinees" of our own invention. The century may have been mistaken and the wrong river may have been explored, but the spirit of adventure was alive and well.

One of the best ways to nurture that same spirit in the classroom and introduce children to the human drama of history is through creative drama—an alternate way of exploring ideas and situations beyond the printed page. The philosophy of Dorothy Heathcote, a noted English educator, on the "drama of discovery" has greatly influenced my own teaching techniques. Although she advises no preconceived plan, I think a framework for planning and action is necessary for teachers who are inexperienced with the technique and must work within a curriculum. I have developed an adaptable structure for a drama activity relating to social studies that is simple to initiate and manage with a great deal of success.

The classroom of sixth graders and the experiences described here are typical of the children I have worked with and the "treks through time" that I conducted in the Moorhead, Minn., School District #152, with a special grant from the school board. I think that my procedure for a drama activity can serve as a model for any imagined expedition, past, present or future.

The entire group activity involves a 45-minute classroom planning session, an hour and a half expedition to a nearby park and a 45-minute evaluation back in the classroom. Later, additional classroom time is devoted to individual follow-up projects in art, language arts, geography, science and math.

PLANNING SESSION

The first time the children and I meet, I make an announcement: "I am seeking members for an expedition. They must be strong (many hands go up), adventurous (more are added) and reliable.'' The children may not be absolutely certain about being reliable but after a moment's consideration most hands are up and the children are eager to begin.

I explain that together we will be creating a simulation drama about explorers. But instead of presenting our play on a stage or in the classroom, we'll be performing in nearby Gooseberry Park. Then I ask the students what *simulation* means. After a few groping responses, someone says it is making something like another thing.

I suggest that it would be interesting to create a simulation of the journey of Lewis and Clark. We won't be able to portray the entire expedition, but we can concentrate on one episode, scouting teams looking for a winter campsite on the Missouri River.

You will probably want to encourage your students to choose their own favorite explorer. I concentrate on Lewis and Clark because they actually stopped just 200 miles away from our area, and it was one of the best-recorded explorations in American history, an important factor in the follow-up activities.

To determine how much background information the children already have, I ask them what they remember from last year's study of Lewis and Clark. In bits and pieces, they recall that the expedition traveled west and north on the Missouri River seeking a water route to the Pacific Ocean. One boy remembers that the Louisiana Purchase triggered the need for exploration; another knows that Jefferson was our president at the time. But no one remembers that the date of the exploration was 1804–1806.

OBJECTIVES AND JOBS

The students' recollections of the event may not be detailed, but we have enough basic information to begin defining the long-term objectives of the expedition, the immediate goals of the scouting teams and the kinds of jobs that the explorers had to do. Their understanding of these objectives will determine the action of the dramas.

First, I write ''long-term objectives'' on the board and ''water route'' under it. Then I ask the students what else besides a water route the explorers were looking for and what they think President Jefferson's instructions were. I usually get an assortment of answers, such as ''information about terrain,'' ''available water,'' ''kinds of wildlife in the area'' and ''the soil.'' I classify these as ''scientific information,'' the second long-term objective.

I suggest a third purpose of the trip: ''the need to locate near a friendly Native American nation'' in order to set up trade, to get information about what lay further west and to provide mutual protection against attack. The children are not familiar with the facts behind this objective, so I briefly explain that Lewis and Clark knew the Mandan Native Americans lived in our area but weren't sure if they would be friendly.

To zero in on the immediate objectives, I ask the students what necessary things a scouting team would be searching for to set up a winter campsite so far north in the wilderness. The children are beginning to get caught up in the excitement of our plans, so they answer quickly: "wood for shelter and fires, water, food and friendly Native Americans."

The third part of our planning session concerns jobs. First, the children's classroom teacher divides them into teams of six members each. Then I solicit their ideas on how we should set up the tasks that will best meet our objectives and goals. With some help from me, they settle on: hunting, scouting, wood gathering, cooking, quartermastering (allotting food and clothing), log keeping, leading, mapmaking, interpreting, drawing, flag bearing and collecting scientific information.

IMAGINARY ACTION

Once we have established the goals and jobs, we talk about the kind of drama we're trying to create. I ask the children what part or parts will be real, and they readily respond: "The trees, the river, the weather." I add two other real things by informing them that each team will carry a bright-colored flag to stake out its campsite and that I will furnish real food.

Then I ask, "What parts must be imaginary?" Someone usually answers, "What happens to us on the expedition." This helps me to explain that the "action" of drama, or the tasks the children choose, must be invented.

Another imaginary part of our drama is the way in which time is manipulated. I explain that the expedition will last only an hour and a half in real time, but their drama will represent two days. This will allow the children to enact camping out overnight, gathering around an imaginary fire for warmth, appointing a sentry, etc.

The last item we talk about before the students meet in teams is how the explorers will respond to internal or external problems. I inform them that they can expect visits to their campsites from strangers. If the visitors are wearing white headbands, they are messengers from the base camp (me) delivering a problem to be solved by the group. If they are wearing red headbands, they represent Native Americans.

In our project these roles were taken over by student teachers, but they could just as easily be played by student volunteers. I ask the children how they think they should react to the Native Americans. The students agree that they must be very careful not to provoke hostilities.

Now each team meets to organize its tasks. Planning is fairly noisy, but rapid, as the children decide who will take what roles. Since there are more tasks than members, some children take on two or three roles. The chosen roles plus the objectives sufficiently suggest the action of the drama so that further instructions are unnecessary. After all, the children are going to be discoverers, searching for all kinds of experiences and knowledge, not knowing in advance what they will find. This condition is essential to build their anticipation and excitement.

ON THE TRAIL

The next day the children, their teacher, the student teachers and I pile into several cars and drive to Gooseberry Park—an ideal location for our adventures, since it covers 10 acres on an oval peninsula reaching out into the Red River. There is good tree shelter all the way around, about 50 to 100 yards from the riverbank.

I distribute flags and provisions (candy bars) and give some final instruction. After a quick reminder about individual duties, cooperation, safety and goals, we move backward in time to November 13, 1804.

I role play a minor lieutenant issuing orders to signal that the drama has begun: "Members of the expedition! Can you hear me? We have ascended the Missouri River as far north as we can for this season. The river will soon be frozen. So we must seek out a winter campsite where we can survive in this rugged wilderness until the coming of spring. We need timber for shelter, game for food and fresh water. Probably most important of all, we must locate a friendly Native American tribe for trade and mutual protection. Our very survival may depend on this.

"We know we're close to the Mandan settlements, but we have not spotted them yet. So be alert! Under no circumstances provoke hostilities. Remember your duties, be steadfast in pursuit of our goals, brave in the face of danger, loyal to each other and to our president, Thomas Jefferson!"

I then send each team off in a different direction, with their leaders in the forefront. They are on their own, for better or worse, for the next hour and 30 minutes.

All the teams seem to settle on an initial campsite very quickly. Their colored flags help their teacher and me spot them in the woods and keep some track of their movements.

As a dispatcher and receiver of reports, I stay under a park shelter— our "base camp." Occasionally a team sends a runner back with a message or discovered object, real or imagined. But most make no attempt to communicate.

PROBLEM SOLVING

Our messengers begin their rounds after about 15 minutes, dispatching the problems in the form of handwritten messages that each team has to resolve. These are based on situations that were a part of the original expedition so that we can later compare the team solutions to what actually happened. The problems not ony help to focus the children's attention on a situation that the original explorers dealt with, but also provide some material for improvisation.

Some of the difficulties involve internal breakdowns, such as a deserter stealing provisions and trying to escape, a member breaking a leg or the group suffering from severe frostbite. Other problems concern external threats such as a grizzly bear or a buffalo herd approaching the campsite.

The messengers report that the children's involvement is generally very strong. With little instruction, the students respond to and maintain the imagined situations very well. "Hunters" search for game, "cooks" devise wilderness meals, "artists" draw pictures of the setting and so on.

The arrival of Native Americans is anticipated with great excitement. The student teachers try to approach the campsites stealthily, but it's hard to surprise the watchful sentries and scouts. To communicate with the interpreters, the Native Americans pantomime a variety of simple ideas, such as the Shoshone greeting described by Lewis, the need for food and shelter and the desire to trade articles. The explorers readily understand and respond with impromptu sign language.

RETURN TO HOME BASE

When time is up, I blow a whistle, and the explorers tramp out of the woods. I ask for quick impressions from each team, and then we return to school for further reports. In the classroom, a ragged assortment of sticks, bones and rocks are displayed by the "scientists." I ask each team to report on the solutions to its problems, and we compare notes from the real logs of Lewis and Clark about how they solved similar dilemmas. For example, in the case of frostbite, the children learned to their discomfort that on the original expedition, the affected fingers and toes were amputated.

We also listened to the log keepers read their reports. Here are the unedited field notes, written on the march, of one team's log keeper:

"November 13, 1804. A glooming day, cold patches of snow, no sign of indians. we seen smoke signals over the trees, saw indian tracks, we got a deer the first day the hide will be used for shelter. indians are coming up from the front they weren't friendly. our best guide stoled our food. (We gave her a chance to live because we needed her help) move to find water.

"Next day. indian liked shelly's yellow hair. We saw a hill with water. scout saw an owl. (It was a real owl) it was heavy wood area. we went fishing. saw a dead fish. Scouts saw a heard of bofflo, got bofflo, got deer and buck. Have enough food. carry food with us."

After the logs are read aloud, I read what Lewis and Clark wrote in their logs about the same time. Everyone listens intently.

"11th November Sunday 1804. Fort Mandan. [Clark] Continued at work at the Fort Two men cut themselves with an ax. The large ducks pass to the South an Indian gave me several rolls of parched meat two squars of the Rock mountains, purchased from the Indians by a frenchman came down with the Mandans out hunting the Buffalow" (From *The Journals of Lewis and Clark* by Bernard De Voto. Houghton-Mifflin.)

"Monday 19. [Lewis] The ice continues to float in the river, the wind high from the northwest, and the weather cold. Our hunters arrived from their excursion below, and bring a very fine supply of thirty-two deer, eleven elk, and five buffaloe, all of which was hung in a smokehouse." (From *The Lewis and Clark Expedition* by Meriwether Lewis. Lippincott.)

The children are amazed! Without being told in advance, they had invented the very same situations. They immediately saw a link between themselves and the long-dead explorers because of the experiences they had in common. After hearing as many reports as I can in 30 to 40 minutes, I share pictures about the real expedition from the book *In the Footsteps of Lewis and Clark* by Gerald Snyder (National Geographic Society).

I also show the students a few real items that might have been part of the event, such as authentic Native American snowshoes and a basket and the skeletons and feathers of a mallard duck and a Canadian snow goose, and a packet of additional enrichment materials that I have compiled based on my own research on the event. This includes lists of supplies and Native American gifts, accounts from the original logs about encounters with bighorn sheep and grizzlies, maps and sketches and a list of creative follow-up projects.

TRAILBLAZING IDEAS

To carry the children's enthusiasm for exploring a few steps further, I suggest they choose at least one activity from each of the following six

categories. To motivate research, I ask them to imagine that they are
explorers returning to civilization who want to convey as much information
about the new land as possible.

Art

- Draw or paint a picture of one or more of the following: a portrait of a
  Native American leader, a village, the women's or children's activities,
  a buffalo hunt, a tribal ceremony, pictographs, an encounter with a
  grizzly bear, a canoe on the river rapids or in a storm.

Geography

- Create a map in imitation of Native Americans by drawing it on a scrap
  piece of fake leather or constructing a small model.
- Draw your own detailed map of a small section of the river and surround-
  ing land and indicate tree cover, topography, sandbars, river channel,
  etc.

Language Arts

- Tape-record or write an imaginary account of a week's activities by the
  explorers.
- Write a narrative about encounters with Native Americans and include a
  description of their culture.
- Draw pictures of Native American hand language and translate each
  sign.

Science

- Draw charts of planets, constellations and the winter sky and explain
  how they helped you predict what the terrain would be like.
- Write a few paragraphs relating what the Native Americans taught you
  about astronomy.
- Write descriptions of your observations of migratory birds and draw
  illustrations.
- Sketch the skeletal structure and feathers or skins of the most common
  animals and birds.
- Set up a display box of various kinds of rocks and soil and label each
  sample.

Record Keeping

- Compile supply lists and check them against what your scouting team used in a month. (Include Native American gifts.)
- Draw up a chart showing the day-to-day temperature and precipitation for a month and compare it to the weather records in the original logs.

Native American Artifacts

- Construct a peace pipe from any available materials and write a paragraph on its uses.
- Write a detailed description of adult and children's clothing, including the sources of all materials.
- Put together a complete recipe for pemmican.

Within a week or so of the activity, the children are asked to write down their opinions and feelings about their experiences. Here are a few representative comments: "It was so exciting. I never knew what would happen next." "It made me feel so important. . . . " "I never knew what time it was . . . and it really didn't matter." "I really felt like the explorers, walking in their footsteps. . . . "

I conducted similar expeditions with 15 other sixth grades with almost identical results. Although different classes of children used different titles and their actions and solutions to problems varied, they all defined and achieved the same tasks and goals.

I think the primary objective of creative drama is the need to inspire an integrated human response of mind, heart and body all wrapped up into one spontaneous package. In an open setting, without a clock or any walls, my explorers had the freedom and motivation for this total response. They became true members of the community of Meriwether Lewis and William Clark.

Fostering Moral Development through Creative Dramatics

by Gloria Jane Wallin

Piaget (1932) emphasized that children need peer interaction to proceed through the moral stages. DeVries and Kamii (1975) found that the use of group games in the classroom helped bring about moral growth. Way (1967) stressed the need for creative dramatics in the classroom in fostering moral development. This article describes a program of creative dramatics that I designed and implemented in several inner-city schools to foster moral development.

PROGRAM

The children in the project were sixth and seventh graders who had chosen creative dramatics as an elective course. They were experienced in theater games and sensory exercises when the project was initiated. I used Spolin's (1963) approach to creative dramatics. The emphasis was on understanding the individual child and helping her or him give up egocentricity. The dramatics instructor was careful not to force precise patterns of thinking and behavior on the children to allow them to ''grow and unfold in a free atmosphere'' (Spolin, 1963, p. 286). This approach set the tone for what Selman (1976) referred to as role taking (p. 301) in the process of moral development. The youngsters were helped to understand the social reasoning of other people and to relate the social points of view of other people to their own. It was hypothesized that dramatization of the various moral dilemma situations and their resolutions would help the students make the transition from advanced moral judgment to advanced moral behavior.

At the beginning, the moral dilemmas were presented by me. They were taken from *Developing Values* (Guidance Associates, 1973) and *Values in a Democracy* (Guidance Associates, 1976). In groups of three or four, the students rehearsed for about 10 minutes before presenting their dramatization to the class. Each dramatization was videotaped, replayed, and followed by a class discussion. Frequently, the students in the audience expressed different resolutions to the dilemmas. The students were encouraged to examine the reasons behind their resolutions of the dilemmas. After several weeks, the youngsters were given the opportunity to create their own dilemmas. The students developed the following three dramatizations:

Dramatization A

Mary's friend, Joan, comes to visit. They are both 16 years old. Mary's mother is drunk. Joan wants to call the social worker for help. Mary is afraid that the other kids in school will discover that her mother is an alcoholic. Mary's mother finishes the bottle of liquor and flings it across the room. Joan dials the telephone and Mary's mother screams. The social worker arrives and calls for an ambulance. Mary's mother has collapsed.

One week later, Mary calls Joan and thanks her for making the call to the social worker. She agrees that they should have sought help earlier but she was embarrassed.

Dramatization B

Sharon, age 15, and her mother are having a discussion. Mother begs Sharon not to have a sexual relationship with her boyfriend. She explains that she was 15 when she gave birth to Sharon, and she wants something better for her daughter. She wants Sharon to go to college. Sharon insists that her mother doesn't understand her. They agree to discuss it with the "lady" at the Family Planning Center.

Dramatization C

Kathy's mother beats her for not having her report card. Kathy insists that her grades were good but that Stephanie stole her report card. Mother agrees to go to Stephanie's house to get her daughter's report card. Stephanie refuses to let her in. When Stephanie's mother comes home, she talks with Kathy's mother. Kathy's mother realizes that Stephanie has shown her mother the stolen report card. She is also aware that Stephanie's sister is very sick in the hospital, and the family does not need any new problems. She asks to see Stephanie's report card, and tells her mother the truth.

CONCLUSION

Peer interaction in the classroom can make an important contribution to the moral development of the child. The creative dramatics approach is a way of encouraging this interaction so that youngsters develop the ability to make moral judgments. Insofar as they themselves dramatize their moral judgments, the link to advanced moral behavior may be strengthened.

REFERENCES

DeVries, R., and Kamii, C. *Why Group Games? A Piagetian Perspective.* Urbana, IL: University of Illinois Publications, 1975.

Piaget, Jean. *The Moral Judgment of the Child.* Translated by M. Gabain. New York: The Free Press, 1965.

Selman, R.L. "Social-Cognitive Understanding: A Guide to Educational and Clinical Practice." In *Moral Development and Behavior*, edited by Thomas Liekona, et al. New York: Holt, Rinehart, and Winston, 1976.

Spolin, Viola. *Improvisation for the Theatre.* Evanston, IL: Northwestern University Press, 1963.

Way, Brian. *Development through Drama.* Atlantic Highlands, NJ: Humanities Press, 1967.

Two Hits with One Throw: Drama and Values

Take my hand, come with me
Where the children are free . . . [1]

These words are from a song that represents a creative approach to the
curriculum of 7th and 8th grade classes of a middle school. Three hundred
students in one semester had the opportunity to assess and change personal
values through drama and music.

Teaching values in the classroom has often been either a hit or miss
operation or misused as an opportunity to preach one's own values. Since in
our culture, we believe individuals have a right to their own set of values,
others feel it is presumptuous to include values in any curriculum course.
However, there are two standard values for most people in our society: a
belief in the basic worth of the individual and a belief in rationality. The first
area will develop within children in the home environment and can sometimes be influenced by the manner teachers and others relate to the children.
The latter area,

> rational processes—avoiding premature judgment, collecting and weighing
> evidence, evaluating alternative conclusions—can be practiced and refined
> in the classroom. Furthermore, rationality can provide a sound basis for the
> student to evaluate what "ought to be" for himself. This is an essential skill;
> for in a changing world, no generation has all the answers for its successors. [2]

If people are going to have an opinion in any communication situation,
they need to have their own value foundations. Teachers are familiar with
the passive student who has risked nothing in absorbing world sophistication from a TV screen but has not had an equal development time to
establish a value system which can sift out stable points for the student's
life. This middle school experience exposed students to new ways of
looking at friendships, sexual roles, family relationships, politics and most
important of all: themselves.

Many sources of material were used, but the major emphases were from the work of Marlo Thomas' *Free to Be You and Me* and the Broadway production *The Me Nobody Knows* (based on the book of the same title using original writing of children from the New York ghetto).[3] Our culminating production was entitled *Free to Be The You and Me That Nobody Knows*. The preparation that took place in the classroom, rather than the actual performance, however, was the important part. Material was compiled and sorted by what the students felt relevant. Evaluative small group discussions were held, and then roleplaying of problems and situations that the discussions initiated. We also used creative dramatics for the stories in *Free to Be You and Me,* along with other value-packed stories. Nellie McCaslin in *Creative Dramatics in the Classroom* states: "A well-planned session in creative dramatics provides exercises in critical thinking as well as an opportunity for creativity."[4] Individual oral interpretation was used as we searched to identify attitudes of others in excerpts from *The Me Nobody Knows* plus poetry collected or written by the students. The most meaningful selections were compiled into a single book and copies were made. This minibook provided practice material to develop skills in the mechanics of oral interpretation. By time of production, it was easy to choose the final selections as definite favorites had emerged.

These activities were in speech and drama classes. However, the diverse content would have been possible in language arts or even social studies (our 7th graders had a unit that provided a good relationship to the material). The music classes discussed content of the songs with other value education material. They worked on movement that would express mood behavior.

The structure of the final production was loose, using singing, movement, creative dramatics and oral interpretation. There was a theme division into four parts, which reflected the classroom studies.

The Introduction pictured everyone as a unique individual that has a special contribution to the world. A pantomime opened the show with the song, "The Tree." A man plans to cut down an apple tree because it never bears apples. A heavy fog saves the tree from extinction and the next day a baby apple appears. The stem of that apple becomes the narrator, reminding us throughout the performance, that life is precious. The entire cast enters wearing masks, singing and moving to "Free to Be You and Me." When a reader says, "The world will be a different place because of me . . . Let the world be a better place because I am!", all the students removed their masks and shouted, "I am!" The poetry and singing of this section ends with the song Jim Croce made famous, "I Got a Name."[5]

The second part pertained to the way we all have different and yet common experiences in growing up. Creative dramatics revealed new babies in the hospital and their parents' dreams for them. The script continued with what happens when some people think their "special place in life" sets them above others; it also included scenes of the identity crisis in the roles of a boy who wants a doll, times when it is alright to cry, and the threats of growing up.

The skits, songs and poetry in the third section concentrated on the fact that we make choices in how we spend each day. The drama demonstrated different ways families start the day, the cliques at the bus stop and the day in the classroom. Material for the latter had as a base, chapter one of *Up the Down Staircase,*[6] by Bel Kaufman, and was supported with other material. The whole section emphasized the decisions we must make in behavior and goals. "The Book Report" from *Charlie Brown*[7] added insight and comedy.

The last part of the theme brought out other influences on our lives through the media. Humor and pathos were expressed on the problems of the energy crisis, crime, the generation gap, drugs, minority conflicts, hunger and loneliness.

The finale began with e. e. cummings' words:

> To be nobody-but-yourself—in a world which is doing its best, night and day, to make you everybody else—means to fight the hardest battle which any human being can fight; and never stop fighting.

The rest of the script emphasized this idea in poetry, movement and song as the students strived to be *Free to Be the You and Me That Nobody Knows*.

Values cannot be easily tested for a final evaluation but so many students made statements of what the experience had meant to them; parents phoned, wrote, or told the teachers personally of attitude changes; that all felt goals had been accomplished. The criteria for the process of valuing according to Raths, Harmin, and Simon[8] were met:

1. *Choosing freely*
   There was no coercion to accept any of the proposed ideas.
2. *Choosing from among alternatives*
   Different choices were discussed and decisions were up to the students.
3. *Choosing after thoughtful consideration of the consequences of each alternative*
   The entire process was worked on at various times during the semester with the final concentration in four weeks. This gave ample time to think through many of the ideas.
4. *Prizing and cherishing*
   Students were pleased to share the values they felt important.
5. *Affirming*
   The repetition of the final class choices for the production and the

wanting to share the ideas with as many as possible supported this
component.

6. *Acting upon choices*

As stated earlier actual changes in behavior were noted by the students
themselves and parents.

7. *Repeating*

It could not be judged if the recognized values: new, changed or
re-enforced would persist. However, one boy, when a show was being
considered the next year, wanted to know if the theme would help him to
grow personally like the year before.

A test of the idea came the next year when another county school used
some of the same basic value education material. Without music, they
worked up their own successful production. A production would not even
be necessary to achieve the goal of developing rational processes and value
judgments. The curriculum in any speech, language arts, or social studies
course could include these oral activities for the benefit of the students.
Next time you plan drama, make it drama and values!

NOTES

1. Fran Klagsburn, Editor. *Free to Be You and Me*. N.Y.: McGraw
Hill Co., 1974. Music—Carole Hart, Stephen Lawrence, and Bruce Hart.
Free to Be You and Me (with Marlo Thomas). N.Y.: A & R Studios.

2. Marion Brady and Howard L. Brady. *A Rationale for Social
Studies*. Florida Dept. of Education, 1971.

3. Stephen M. Joseph, Editor. *The Me Nobody Knows*. New York:
Avon Books, 1969. Music—Gary Wm. Friedman, Will Holt, and Herb
Schapiro. *The Me Nobody Knows*. Sunbeam Music Inc., 1970.

4. Nellie McCaslin. *Creative Dramatics in the Classroom*. Revised
Edition, N.Y.: David McKay Company, Inc., 1974.

5. Norman Gimbel and Charles Fox. "I Got a Name." Los Angeles:
Fox Fanfare Music, Inc., 1973.

6. Bel Kaufman. *Up the Down Staircase*. Englewood Cliffs, N.J.:
Prentice-Hall Inc., 1964.

7. Clark Gesmer. "Book Report" from *Charlie Brown*. New York:
Jeremy Music Inc., 1965.

8. Louis E. Raths, Merrill Harmin, and Sidney B. Simon. *Values and
Teaching: Working With Values in the Classroom*. Columbus, Ohio:
Charles E. Merrill Publishing Co., 1966.

PART V
Science and Career Education

Introductory Comments

Both science and career education must draw on the past, the present, and the future to encourage student participation. The articles in this section display the ways teachers have combined the unique qualities found in drama with science and career education to involve students in discovering the natural world around them and in investigating possible future occupations.

Alfred A. Arth and J. Howard Johnston supply the reader with a rationale for "Dramatization and Gaming for Optimum Environmental Survival" to be used with a wide age span. Objectives, materials for the game, procedure, activity worksheet, and a list of organizations interested in environmental awareness are given.

Elwanda Lu Conley uses humorous skits and "news broadcasts" to introduce nutrition to students. Her article, "How I Teach Nutrition," lists examples of items occurring on "The Six O'Clock News" and shows how fun and learning can be combined to heighten student interest.

In an attempt to increase the number of students who take physics and to make the subject more visible within the curriculum, Richard Lee Ponting found an answer by "Combining Physics and Drama." He shares his ideas of combining analytical thinking with dramatization, and his successful experience includes a variety of activities.

Katherine Y. B. Yao and Eleanor A. Kelly describe a program which utilizes dramatization in providing career awareness to children in "Integrating Science with the Creative Arts in Career Education." While the creative dramatics idea here is incorporated especially in the area of science, it also involves other areas of the curriculum as well. Finally, "Creative Dramatics for Teaching Career Concepts to the Young Child," by Thomas D. Yawkey and Eugene L. Aronin, describes those attributes of creative dramatics which assist in developing a program in career education.

Dramatization and Gaming for Optimum Environmental Survival

by Alfred A. Arth and J. Howard Johnston

Recently, the educational system has found another noble crusade, a safe cause with which to align itself, that of ecological salvation. In pursuing this noble cause, the schools have been fair game for those whose aims may be somewhat less than altruistic. The result has been a deluge of "ecological" films, slides, posters, buttons, bumper stickers, and programmed learning packages. Motivated by an apparent guilt constructed on a lack of exposure combined with that ambiguous feeling of past failure and perpetuated by the byline seeking environmental specialists, the faculties of public schools have purchased great volumes of ecological materials as a panacea for their hastily formed ecological clubs or newly instituted environmental education programs.

In so doing, we, as a profession, appear to have ignored as a teaching resource the very immediate environment we have pledged to save. Since the exact ecological catastrophe appears at least as ambiguous as the guilt attached to the ignorance of its existence, it seems that we should tap those resources which surround us and look to the environment itself for discovering the logical structure to protect it; a structure which will provide for the logic of an ecological awareness.

There is a certain element of regionalism which the manufacturers of "scare tactic" films have failed to recognize. Showing films of suds-laden rivers, coastal oil spills, and poisonous clouds of haze hanging over a skyline does not evoke the same immediacy reaction from a child in Wyoming as it might in California, Missouri, or Massachusetts. This is not to imply that the ecological balance in Wyoming is any less fragile than that of a more populous state, only that such gross pollution is viewed as a remote possibility in those essentially unspoiled states.

What follows is a proposed lesson which builds upon observation and dramatization to make its environmental point. Granted, a "game" of sorts is used, but it is an integral part of the dramatization lesson, teacher constructed, and available for the cost of postage. This exercise has been used with first graders, junior high school principals, seventh graders, and high school conservation groups, so that with only slight modification it might be used by virtually any age group.

The following material is a possible usage plan for the above mentioned concepts.

OBJECTIVES

1. To provide the participant with the skills necessary to view the natural environment as an interrelated sum of component parts, each dependent upon the other for optimum survival.
2. To provide the participant with the skills necessary to develop a clear and accurate structure of the natural eco-system through participation in a dramatization of the life supporting system.
3. To provide the child with the skills necessary to see that the environment is a physical reality with depth and scope and not a remote abstract term.

MATERIALS FOR "YOU ARE" GAME

1. Any interactional area—a school yard, park, pond, forest, lawn, parking lot, etc. Whatever is readily available.
2. A 3×5 card for each member of the group, upon which is written, "You are _____", with the blank space filled by one of the following:

You are . . .

the sun	a berry	a frog
a rock	a tree	a chicken
the wind	a leaf	an owl
rain	a log	a bird
hail	a flower	a hawk
a stream	a worm	a fox
soil	a fly	a mouse
a swamp	a flea	a rabbit
a seed	a lady-bug	an automobile
grass	a bee	a road
a berry bush	a fish	a rusty beer can*

*This is the normally expected order of development, but students may be able to justify an alternate pattern.

If additional cards are needed, the teacher may use supplements from within the basic sequence. Some suggested areas from which additional elements might be constructed are:

Trees: hardwood and softwood
Marsh growth: cattails, pussywillows
Warmblooded animals: gopher, squirrel
Coldblooded animals: reptiles, turtles

PROCEDURE

1. Take the group outside and give the following directions:
   - You may not communicate with each other in any way.
   - Look around you at signs of the natural environment. You may walk about or sit in one spot. You might wish to look closely at a leaf, a blade of grass, a tree, the sky, or any other natural object which captures your interest.
2. After fifteen minutes have passed, bring the participants back to the classroom to discuss their findings. The instructor might ask each participant if he would give to the group a brief description of the object he studied. The participants should also be encouraged to share with the group any sensory perceptions which they developed as a result of this exercise. For example: "What do you now know about your object that you did not know before?" Every participant should be given the opportunity to present an idea to the group.
3. After the discussion has been completed, give each participant a 3×5 card bearing one of the "You are _____" sentences. Tell them to leave these cards face-down until the game begins.
4. Tell the participants that they are going to build our planet. The participants themselves will act as all of the elements necessary, and the model will be constructed by lining the group up in the order that the elements normally appear through natural evolution.
5. Ask, "Who goes first?" Normally, the response will be "the sun," since all life systems need energy to evolve. It must be stressed here that the instructor acts only as a guide, asking the kinds of subtle questions that will lead the participants to the discovery of the seemingly proper order. If one of the elements is left out, the individual who holds that card will soon realize that the evolution process has passed him and he will be quick to remedy the omission, either by squeezing into his "slot" or by asking where he belongs.

6. As the line builds, the instructor should encourage each person to re-evaluate his own position in terms of his importance to the rest of the system. In addition, he should ask the participants to consider the importance of each element as it is added to the chain, "Why is the log important to me, a lady-bug?"

7. When the line is completed, three participants should be left out of the line: "the road," "the automobile," and "the rusty beer can." The instructor should then call for the three remaining persons to join the line and say, "If this interactional structure existed on several acres of land, what elements of this chain would be endangered or eliminated by the addition of a road? If you think you would be among this group removed by the road, sit down." The results of this statement are most dramatic since over ⅔ of the participants, those holding the stream, swamp, seed, grass, berry bush, berry, tree, leaf, log, flower, worm, fish, frog, flea, lady-bug, bee, chicken, owl, bird, hawk, fox, mouse, and rabbit cards, will leave the line. The instructor should then question those who remain and ask why they would be unaffected. Once this activity is completed, the participants return to their seats and a follow-up discussion and activity begins.

8. *Follow-up*
   A. Discussion Questions
      1. Can we do away with roads?
      2. How could we design a road that would remove a minimal amount of the natural environment?
      3. What can *we* do to help protect the type of system we have created here?
   B. Writing-talking activity
      Work sheet

   Variable Activity Worksheet

   You Are _____

   A. If you were in a shadow box scene:
      1. How would you be placed in sequence with the other things?
      2. How would you be valued in relation to the other things?
      3. Who would be in the scene first?
      4. What would your size be compared to the other things?
      5. Do people like you?

   B. If you were in a real life scene:
      1. How fast would you move compared to the others?
      2. Whom would you stay away from?

  3. How many of you would there be in one acre?

  4. Whom do you help the most?

  5. What do you feel like?

  6. Where do you go at night?

C. Carry Over

  1. Write a limerick with ecology as a theme.

  2. Write a story, pretending you are one of the objects in the life system the class built.

  3. Write a letter to a Senator or Representative, expressing your concern for the environment.

  4. Working in a group, write a short play in which the characters are objects in the environment.

  5. Draw a graph or picture of a food chain.

  By way of conclusion, it might be of some interest to compare the reactions of elementary and junior high school aged children with those of adult participants.

  Both groups were able to conceptualize the model with some accuracy. This is evidenced by the fact that the "chain" was built rapidly and with a minimum of hesitation on the part of those involved in the exercise. The children, however, were more apt to aid each other in finding a place in the developmental line. In addition, the children seemed more willing to question a sequence which they thought was inaccurate or which they did not understand. This observation might be attributed to the fact that children have not acquired the same sequence relationship sophistication as the adults, or by the simple fact that the gamelike nature of the activity may have greater appeal for children.

  In response to the question, "How could you build a road which removes a minimum amount of the natural environment?" the responses from the children seemed to be more creative than the suggestions of the adults. While the adults were inclined to suggest medians and dividers to preserve at least some of the natural setting, the children suggested air cars which require no highway at all, travel by light beam, etc. This seems to indicate that the children were less burdened by a notion of what is "impossible," one of the more pronounced characteristics of maturity.

  While a design engineer may shudder at some of the children's more visionary solutions, one cannot deny the merits of brainstorming. This type of activity might serve us well in breaking down some of the old barriers of "practicality" and "pragmatism" spawned not of experimentation, but neglect.

  This modern era with its flashing computer lights and the necessity for getting from point A to point B as rapidly as possible leaves contemporary

American man no time for the luxurious perception of the environment that lies in between. There appears to be a paramount need to provide our concerned citizenry with the skills necessary to observe those life space activities that exist around them at all times. Possible solutions to our environmental concerns are readily available and these provident individuals must be assisted with their development of the very basic environmental equation: Awareness, Commitment, and Responsible Action. No meaningful action can ever come about until the logic of awareness has been established.

What follows is a list of some of those organizations which share in the concern for developing this awareness.

[Editors' note: the reader is encouraged to write to the organizations listed for current prices and availability of the materials before ordering.]

1. The Izaak Walton League of America
   1326 Waukegan Road
   Glenview, Illinois 60025
   A membership organization with local chapters and state divisions; also national memberships. Promotes conservation of renewable natural resources and development and protection of high quality outdoor recreation opportunities. Chapters and divisions can furnish speakers and literature. Publishes monthly Izaak Walton Magazine. Maintains a Conservation Office at 719 13th St., NW, Washington, D.C. 20005.

2. Clean Water—It's Up To You
   A citizen's guide to clean water action; available free from Izaak Walton League, (see above).

3. Keep America Beautiful, Inc.
   99 Park Avenue
   New York, NY 10016
   A national nonprofit, public service organization for the prevention of litter and for the enhancement of urban and rural scenic and man-made beauty. Publishes helpful brochures and newsletters on litter prevention.

4. Natural Science for Youth Foundation
   763 Silvermine Road
   New Canaan, Connecticut 06840
   Helps communities set up natural science centers, wildlife preserves, and trailside museums for involving young people first hand with the world of nature.

5. Catalog of Federal Domestic Assistance
   A definitive listing and explanation of all federal assistance programs.

Available free from the Information Center, Office of Economic
Opportunity, Executive Office of the President, Washington, D.C.
20506.

6. Conservation Directory
   Listing of principal national and state organizations, public and private. $1.50 a copy. Published by National Wildlife Federation, 1412
   16th Street, NW, Washington, D.C. 20036.

7. County Action for Outdoor Recreation
   Forty-eight page guide on practical steps for county park and recre-
   ational programs. Available for 25¢ a copy from the National Association of Counties, 1001 Connecticut Avenue, NW, Washington, D.C.
   20036.

8. A Little About Lots
   Excellent manual on how to make vest pocket parks of vacant lots,
   organize tree planting and neighborhood clean-up programs. 50¢—
   available from the Park Association of New York City, 15 Gramercy
   Park South, New York, NY 10003.

9. Zero Population Growth
   416 East Jefferson Street
   Charlottesville, Virginia 22901
   Phone: 295-1000
   Free use of filmstrips, paperbacks, free memberships in the Kindness
   Club, and numerous free pamphlets on the population problem.

10. Kindness Club
    Waterford, Virginia
    Teacher manual, monthly newsletter for students; Charlottesville
    Z.P.G. will underwrite the cost for each class (see above address).

11. The Editors, *American Home*
    641 Lexington Avenue
    New York, NY 10022
    "24 Insignificant Ways to Cause a Significant Change" (No charge).
    An excellent poster giving ways the public can aid in combating
    pollution in their own home environment.

12. Conservation Foundation
    1250 Connecticut Avenue, NW
    Washington, D.C. 20036
    Variety of pamphlets and articles dealing with the many aspects of
    ecology.

13. American Association of University Women
    2401 Virginia Avenue, NW
    Washington, D.C. 20037

Resource directory on pollution control, 75¢
Anti-pollution pamphlets and study guide, 75¢

14. Environmental News
    E.P.A.
    Office of Public Affairs
    Washington, D.C. 20460
    A free newsletter which keeps one informed of the activities of the
    E.P.A. (Environmental Protection Agency).

15. Ranger Rick
    National Wildlife Federation
    1412 16th Street, NW
    Washington, D.C.
    Experiments and lesson plans illustrating various ecological concepts,
    free teacher's guide, student copy once a month, total cost $6.00.

16. The Garden Club of America
    598 Madison Avenue
    New York, NY 10022
    A national organization representing numerous local garden clubs.
    Active at the local level in beautification, conservation, and open space
    planning. Distributes a free conservation, and open space planning
    packet, "The World Around You."

17. A Nature Center for Your Community
    A basic handbook on the values, objectives, elements, and costs of a
    community nature center and how to go about establishing one. $1.00 a
    copy. National Audubon Society, 1130 Fifth Avenue, New York, NY
    10028.

18. Scientist's Institute for Public Information
    30 West 68th Street
    New York, NY 10021
    Provides public with scientific information on environmental
    problems.

19. Planned Parenthood-World Population
    515 Madison Avenue
    New York, NY 10022
    Free literature on the problems of over-population and methods for
    controlling population.

20. Citizens for Clean Air
    40 West 57th Street
    New York, NY 10019
    Provides posters and information on cleaner air.

21. Conservation Education Association
    1250 Connecticut Avenue
    Washington, D.C. 20036
    Will provide education programs, newsletters, bibliography on con-
    servation education.
22. Director, National Park Service
    U.S. Department of Interior
    Washington, D.C. 20240
    Excellent materials relating to: Preservation Programs, 50¢; National
    Environmental Study Areas, No Charge; and National Environmental
    Education Development.

How I Teach Nutrition

by Elwanda Lu Conley

I've found that one of the best ways to introduce nutrition to students is to get them involved—in writing skits, "news broadcasts," and songs. I give them the idea and a good supply of reference books and then let them dig out the information that they need for their projects. Here are some of the projects that work well.

A Beverly Hillbillies skit, featuring the familiar TV characters, helped teach nutrition and created much interest for my first-year home economics students. I wrote the first act to the skit and then asked a group of students, who enjoy writing and acting, to write the second act. This is a good activity to use when other students are planning or preparing meals. The only requirement is that the second act must be written in hillbilly style, and must contain many true facts about nutrition. I provided these students with many nutrition books that contained the concepts that I wanted to teach. In order to write the second act, the students had to do some reading; but with this method, there was a purpose for reading. The fun came when the skit was presented to the class.

In my first act, I tried to include as many nutrition facts as possible, but in a humorous way to create interest and increase learning. The skit featured Jethro explaining the important nutrition facts that he had learned from an attractive "cookin'"teacher who had moved next door. Granny was not too happy when Jethro told her that she was "cookin'" her "viddles" in too much water, and at too high a temperature. Jethro's excitement became even more intense when he decided that poor eyesight may have been the reason for the lost Watergate tapes; and he was sure that after his letter reached Washington, telling the President about the importance of vitamin A for good eyesight, that he would become a personal advisor and a special companion to Mr. Kissinger. The scene ended with a knock at the door. The students' imagination will determine who is knocking at the door.

Students enjoy dressing up for this skit too. To give them enough time to dress, plan to include the "six o'clock news" between acts. This is another creative activity that the students enjoy. Divide the other members of the class into three or four groups and ask each group to select one member to imitate some news reporter. As a group they'll write the news, telling about some tragic event that has happened to teachers, friends, or famous TV personalities. These tragic events are to have happened because of some neglect in nutrition. My students came up with news like this:

> High winds entered the Chapmanville area today, forcing many residents to evacuate their homes. One eighty-year-old man was so excited that he streaked through the main street of town. Free boxes of cereal will be given out at the courthouse, with the hope that the vitamin B in this food will help settle the nerves of the people in this community. But those who have been consuming raw cabbage, strawberries, and citrus fruits need not worry as much, for if they do get some cuts and bruises, their wounds will heal quickly. As you know, the vitamin C in these foods acts quickly to heal wounds.

> Mayor Fletcher Barker has urged residents in the Chapmanville area to consume all liquids from their canned vegetables for there is a severe water shortage in this area. The people in this community should become very healthy from drinking all of these liquids containing many vitamins and minerals; but the mayor is somewhat worried that residents can't adjust to bathing in this liquid. In any case, we hope for some rain in this area soon so that bathing will become more pleasant.

> An English teacher had much difficulty climbing the stairs this morning to her third floor classroom. She seemed to suffer from severe pains in her leg joints. Doctors have advised her to include vitamin C in her diet. Now you can see this teacher snacking anytime during the day on citrus fruits. Students had a party in her honor today, but instead of the usual birthday gifts, she was given several baskets of citrus fruits and a large head of cabbage.

> But the real tragedy occurred today when the principal walked into a telephone pole on his way to school. He suffered cuts and bruises to his face and legs. Lately his eyesight has been failing and he has had much difficulty seeing in the dark. He was rushed to the Logan General Hospital where he received treatment and was advised by doctors to include more vitamin A in his diet. He will be confined to the hospital for three weeks where he will be given a diet rich in green leafy and yellow vegetables and fruits.

For variety in teaching methods, the students will enjoy singing nutrition songs written to some familiar tune. Some of the more creative students may like to write the songs. This is one that we used. Sing it very slowly to the tune, Down in the Valley.

Vitamin C, (Down in the valley) Good as can be. (Valley so low)
I'll drink some orange juice (Hang your head over)
For vitamin C. (Hear the wind blow)

Vitamin C,
It's good for me.
Give me a lemon for vitamin C.

Cuts, wounds, and bruises will go away.
Drink lots of juice with vitamin C.

Vitamin C, Get some today.
Don't leave it open. It'll go away.

And when colds hit you, Make you feel old,
Chase them away with vitamin C.

Instead of the usual demonstration in which the correct method of cooking vegetables is presented, plan some demonstrations using wrong methods. Have one student demonstrate cooking cabbage for a long time, and another cooking cabbage for a short period of time. Then compare the color, flavor, and texture of the cabbage. Seeing and tasting the actual product will help teach the importance of using the correct method—so much better than just talking about the right and wrong methods.

The students will enjoy a test review by playing nutrition games, rather than by just the usual question and answer period.

I have found that a little fun combined with learning will do much to create interest and increase learning.

Combining Physics and Drama

by Richard Lee Ponting

Dürrenmatt's play *The Physicists*[1] was produced as a cooperative project by my physics class and the drama department at Dudley High School. The results of the project were positive and I hope to encourage other physics teachers to consider introducing dramatic components into their work.

During my first year of teaching at Dudley, I realized that physics had low enrollment and poor recognition as an academic area. I sought a method of increasing class size and the visibility of physics in the school curriculum. Also, having recently read about the theories of "left hemisphere/right hemisphere" brain functioning,[2] I sought a class activity that could promote more holistic, intuitive modes of thought. It occurred to me that drama might provide a vehicle to combine artistic and analytical thinking. I also felt the right play could show physics students the importance of history, philosophy, and moral consequence in the development of science. After discussing this idea with Dan Seaman, the drama teacher, we decided that one of the plays for the coming season might be undertaken as a team-taught, interdisciplinary project by our classes. We agreed that every aspect of the production should be open to students from either the physics or drama class. The play *The Physicists* was chosen because it fit my criteria and because Dan felt it was an artistic challenge.[3]

We decided to schedule combined meetings of our classes on Friday afternoons for that semester. Some of this time was spent introducing the production and allowing for auditions and other activities directly related to the play's production. Most of these meetings, however, were used to educate both classes in the scientific and historical background of the play and its characters. Excerpts from *The Ascent of Man*[4] and the film *Einstein*[5] were among many materials presented during Friday class meetings. I decided to supplement the play with two special projects for students who might wish to be involved in the production but not the play itself. One project was the researching and development of selective biographies of Newton and Einstein, the two historical characters in the play. Selectivity was based upon the desire to establish a connection between their lives and the author's sense of dramatic irony and moral dilemma. These biographies were produced by pairs of students, edited, and finally distributed to the audiences at each performance. In a second project a ten-minute slide/ sound show, created by six students, preceded and introduced each performance. It effectively set the mood and received considerable critical acceptance.

Any project or outside activity undertaken in an academic setting can be distracting and counterproductive to basic educational goals if not kept within a proper context.[6,7] A student in a high school physics course should be given an accurate, comprehensive, and thorough introduction to physics. Because discussion of the play was limited to the Friday sessions and because much of the actual production work and all the rehearsal time was scheduled outside school hours, the standard physics curriculum was not interrupted. Moreover, the time used in the Friday meetings presented useful, relevant, and stimulating material to a cross section of high school students, both science and nonscience oriented.

All eight students in my physics class that semester chose involvement in the production over equally available science projects unrelated to the play. I was surprised that three physics students auditioned for and won (in open audition) major roles in the play. Two physics students worked on the set, one as master builder, and the other three physics students were involved in the special projects. The variety in activities available provided a place for everyone. I noted a sense of togetherness develop that semester that I have never before seen in a physics class. The total production as a class activity contributed to a successful semester.

Anonymous questionnaires were distributed to the physics class to elicit subjective responses to the experience. The students overwhelmingly approved of their project. No student rated it poorly or disapproved of the use of time and effort. Moreover, enrollment in physics for the next semester doubled, producing the largest class in recent memory at this school. It seems clear that this approach to the enrichment of a physics curriculum has merit and deserves consideration by teachers at all levels.

NOTES

1. F. Dürrenmatt, *The Physicists*, (Grove Press, New York, 1962).

2. B. Sample, "Educating for Both Sides of the Human Mind," *Science Teacher* 42, 21 (1975).

3. Other plays which were considered included *Galileo* by Bertolt Brecht and *In the Matter of J. Robert Oppenheimer* by Kipphardt Heinar.

4. J. Bronowski, *The Ascent of Man*, (Little, Brown and Co., Boston, 1973).

5. A documentary film available from Time-Life Multimedia.

6. R. Saltman, "Relevance and Schemes vs. Education in the Sciences," *Science Education* 58, 581 (1974).

7. A. Arons, "Educational Practice—An Expert View of Current Trends," *Physics Teacher* 11, 487 (1973).

Integrating Science with the Creative Arts in Career Education

by Katherine Y. B. Yao and Eleanor A. Kelly

Many elementary schools in the nation have begun to develop different approaches to implement career education in their school activities. At Public School 181 of District No. 17 in Brooklyn, New York, a career education program was implemented as an integral part of the curriculum during the 1974–1975 school year. With an interdisciplinary approach, it focused particularly on integrating science with creative arts in developing career units in each class.

The career education program was aimed at having the child make discoveries about the working world and about himself. The activities were geared toward developing: (1) *career awareness*—to help children know the jobs in the different career clusters and recognize the basic skills, training, and knowledge required for various careers, and to help them relate career explorations to their own aptitudes, values, and interests; (2) *education awareness*—to help children apply basic course content and skills to practical, career-related experiences; and (3) *self-awareness*—to help children know more about their capabilities and interests and create a positive self-image for themselves as worthy, participating members of the society.

The career education program was implemented by the joint efforts of the staff and guidance counselors of P.S. 181 and a team of faculty and student-tutors who were engaged in the Performance-Based Undergraduate Program for the Education of Teachers at Brooklyn College. The team assigned to P.S. 181 concentrated on interdisciplinary training in teaching science and creative arts in elementary school. The student-tutors worked closely with classroom teachers in observing and guiding the learning and teaching activities for two mornings a week.

The fall term began with the preparation and presentation of an assembly program called "Career Education—The Need for Learning Science, Art, and Music." It consisted of fifteen playlets and was designed to show a skeptical boy that learning was important for career selection and preparation. The Brooklyn College student-tutors and the classroom teachers guided the children in grades K–5 in writing the scripts and performing the playlets, which depicted what people do in different careers, identifying particularly those central tasks that require understanding and skills related to the different areas in science and the creative arts. For example, the playlet "The Carpenter," presented by first graders, depicted carpenters cutting wood into different sizes and shapes to build things, using simple tools such as hammers, saws, and sanders. The children sang "We Are the Carpenters" using lyrics they composed, which illustrated simple concepts and skills in science and the arts relating to carpentry. The identification, classification, and construction of sizes and shapes, carving techniques, and the use of simple machines were in this way related to job tasks. Children associated the performance of these tasks with what they were actually learning in the classroom; it also helped them realize the need for learning about science and the creative arts.

OTHER PLAYLETS

Other dramatizations presented different jobs from additional career clusters. "The Restaurant" showed the careers involved in running a restaurant; "The New York Hospital" showed a doctor, a nurse, and a laboratory technician at work. "The Circus," "The Painters," "The Farmers," "The Fire Station," "The Reporter," "The Astronaunts and Engineers," and more, are self-explanatory groupings.

For the spring term, a career unit of study in each class was developed that correlated the world of work with social studies topics and was integrated with science, art, and music. It culminated in a Career Education Exhibit in May where all the class projects produced from the career units were presented in dioramas, posters, murals, folders, scroll television, crafts, movies of children dramatizing different careers, and others. We assigned different topics for the career units to each of the grades, as:

Grade 1. *Workers in the Family*
Grade 2. *Community Workers*
Grade 3. *Jobs in Different Climates*
Grade 4. *Comparison of Work—Then and Now*
Grade 5. *Careers—Economic and Geographic Factors*

SUBTOPICS

Guided by the main topics, each class within a grade developed a career unit based on a more specific subtopic. For example, some of the career units developed included:

- Parents Are People Having Different Jobs
- What I Want to Be When I Grow Up
- People in the Community Work to Help One Another
- Jobs on the Farm
- Careers in Television
- Arts and Artists in American Life from 1700s to the Present
- Cloth-Making in the Colonial Times and Now

To introduce each career to the children, the student-tutors and the classroom teachers developed a series of lessons in science, the creative arts, social studies, and other subjects around a career development theme. The lessons introduced the various concepts and skills in these subjects that were applied in different job tasks. For example, science and the creative arts were combined in a fourth-grade unit called "Cloth-Making in Colonial Times and Now." (See box on page 167.)

As part of their learning activities for these lessons, the children collected raw materials for making cloth, wrote compositions, and drew pictures illustrating the sequence of tasks and the tools needed in the process of making cloth. They also discussed and drew posters of other workers involved in the cloth-making industry such as the sheepherder, farmer, cotton picker, weaver, machine designer and operator, fabric and clothing designer, and others. In addition, the children made clothing in miniature for these workers and tie-dye shirts for themselves.

To further guide the children's self-awareness and knowledge of careers, the teachers focused their attention on the following questions:

- What kind of work do people do in different careers?
- What are the knowledge and skills required in different job tasks?
- Where do people in different careers do their work?
- How do people dress for different kinds of work?
- In what types of climates do people work?
- Why is each job important?
- What are the tools used in different jobs?
- What kind of work interests you? Why?
- Would you be able to do the work?
- How does one prepare oneself to do the work?

The career education program implemented at P.S. 181 provided a variety of learning experiences which acquainted the children with the working world and helped them find out who they are, what their interests and potentials are, and how these potentials could be strengthened and utilized. There are many different career possibilities and we explored only a few. The children did see the importance of learning different subjects in school and saw learning as an integral and essential step toward career development. Through reinforcement of their knowledge and skills in science and the creative arts as well as in other subjects, the children were also led to think about methods of inquiry and how they learned. The culminating activities gave children pride in their achievements and motivated them for further learning.

BY-PRODUCTS

Through their participation in the preparation and implementation of the assembly program and the career units, the student-tutors learned to integrate science with the creative arts and other subjects, thus reinforcing their knowledge and skills in unifying and presenting a core program of instruction around a career development theme. Their research experiences enriched their knowledge in science and the creative arts as well as in other subject areas. Working closely with groups of children and classroom teachers also allowed them to grow more confident as future teachers. The involvement of these student-tutors and their supervising instructors with the school administrators, guidance counselors, classroom teachers, and children in carrying out the career education program created a deeper understanding of needs and a closer working relationship between the college and the school.

THE FUTURE

Plans are underway for this year's program to include field trips to local institutions such as the zoo, the botanical gardens, the telephone company, museums, a theatre, a bank, a hospital, and others to find out what kinds of work are involved in running these institutions. Employees of these institutions will talk about what they do in their careers and how they feel about their work. At the same time, the school will invite parents and representatives from these various local institutions to serve as resource persons who will come into the classroom to discuss their jobs, the understandings and skills required for such jobs, and how one can prepare for them. These activities will help children recognize the part an individual plays in the home, the school, and the community, as well as in a career role.

Cloth-Making in Colonial Times and Now

Topic Lesson	Concepts and Skills Introduced
Raw materials needed for making cloth	Material objects: identifying and classifying
Types of clothing	Material objects: comparing and inferring
Cloth-making using spinning wheel and loom in colonial times	Simple machines and their use: identifying and predicting
Cloth-making by automation today	Forms of energy and their application, characteristics, and varieties of design: differentiating and interpreting
Tie-dyeing	Adhesion, mixing, color combinations, shading and toning: measuring and experimenting
Fabric design	Advancements in the technology of printing patterns: color combinations, wood-block printing, brush, crayon, and pencil techniques
Dress design	Influence of culture on dress design: patterns, form and texture, spacing and proportion, sketching, measuring, cutting, and fitting

Creative Dramatics for Teaching Career Concepts to the Young Child

by Thomas D. Yawkey and Eugene L. Aronin

Rapid changes in society have created an urgent need for a re-examination of traditional relationships of the educational system and the working world. Realizing the need for re-examination, the U.S. Office of Education has encouraged public schools to devise creative ways to acquaint children sequentially with the nature of careers and vocations. The elementary school is a significant participant in this effort, for during these years children develop important attitudes and concepts that affect future vocational behavior.

The task of creating approaches to orient children toward the general nature of work, significant work attitudes, human aspects of work, dignity of labor, and job characteristics implies a unique integration of curriculum concepts and specialties as well as modification in traditional ways of presenting material to children. One invaluable approach that involves maximum participation of the child is creative dramatics, for both creative dramatics and vocational development have characteristics which parallel and complement each other.

CREATIVE DRAMATICS: A COMPLEMENT OF CAREER EDUCATION

One complementary characteristic of both creative dramatics and career education is the personal and active involvement of the student. The natural by-product of creative dramatics is that it easily stimulates the involvement of children through modeling and visual presentation. Student involvement and relevant incidents are also important concomitants.

Another complementary feature of creative dramatics with career education is its close relationship to subject areas. Various language arts skills are emphasized which facilitate language growth and development. Because work involves a broad scene of skills, origins, and setting, the intersection between career development and creative dramatics also spans social studies, arithmetic and reading.

Other attributes of creative dramatics as a method of working with career development are:

1. It is spontaneous, imaginative, free play designed to liberate the mind and stimulate the imagination.
2. Creative dramatics emphasizes participation; its chief aim is experience (Siks, 1958). Creative dramatics enriches the life of the child.
3. It also provides new means for viewing problems and situations. Creative dramatics offers group experiences which are rich in fun, excitement, beauty and laughter, and is a satisfying experience for both teacher and children.
4. Finally, a creative dramatics program brings out the best in content subject as well as the best in teacher and student.

THE CREATIVE DRAMATICS PROCESS

The basic requirements for the creative dramatics program are: (1) a group of children; (2) an interested teacher or leader; (3) space large enough to move freely in; and (4) an idea from which to create. Children's interest in dramatics is high. The children can work in one group or in a number of smaller groups. As a rule the group should not contain fewer than eight and no more than sixteen children at any one time (McCaslin, 1968).

The interested teacher must understand the role as leader in the creative dramatics program. It is not the traditional role of teacher in the classroom. Free expression by children is the key-note, but guidance is an important aspect. The leader must develop imagination to be able to stimulate the children. The teacher guides rather than directs and accepts as well as offers. Specialized training is unnecessary, but the interested teacher will prepare through courses, reading or whatever adaptation of individual skills are needed (McCaslin, 1968). Maintaining a positive attitude toward the program and the children is also very important for the teacher, for acceptance and approval lead to the development of self-confidence. This can only be hindered by a negative attitude. Space can easily be found in classrooms for creative dramatics. The children can work around their desks, on them, under them, or they can be moved to one side of the room for a large working space. The large space offers the most in the way of creative expression.

Goals in creative dramatics programs generally include growth in the affective domain as well as vocational content. Several examples of goals that are consistent with creative dramatics and career education programs for children are to: (1) develop an awareness of attitudes needed to be an optimum worker in school and society, (2) develop confidence and creative expression, (3) develop an awareness of work and the worker's performance, (4) develop social attitudes and relationships, (5) move toward greater emotional stability, (6) give experience in thinking on one's feet, and (7) provide an introduction to good literature (Siks, 1958).

The choice of conceptual material in career development should be suited to age and ability of the children. Vocational material suitable for young children includes elements found in their everyday lives. Satisfaction with jobs and essential job characteristics can be observed in familiar school workers. Attitudes of cooperation and dependability are demonstrated through student-enacted scenes, for example, construction workers building a house. Imaginations can effectively be utilized by having students imagine the work of astronauts. Other vocational ideas for activities in creative dramatics include:

1. a trip on the bus or plane
2. exploring the supermarket
3. a trip to the circus
4. workers in the past
5. father, mother, grandparent
6. farm worker

Creative dramatics usually stimulates much discussion and questioning. Much insight into career concepts can be gained. Does everyone enjoy working? How does one get into a job? Is one kind of job "better" than another? Can working be fun? These questions related to career education can be effectively answered at this time. It is important to explore the feelings and attitudes of the workers, the human elements as well as descriptions of job settings. Workers are people. Since all people are different, so differences exist in motivation, interests, and other factors relating to job choice. People have different jobs because their interests and lifestyles vary. Creative dramatics is one of the best ways to get career education ideas across when used with thoughtful discussion. Include questions which help children recognize achievement of objectives and accompanying feelings in each experience and/or specific lesson. Some examples (from Woods, 1971, p. 15) include:

1. Whom did you see . . . that recognized fears (or honesty, personal commitment, pride, etc.) but accepted the responsibility?
2. How many of you had a feeling of . . . ? Why?

Teachers can develop other questions for evaluation around curiosity about what workers do for recreation, or why workers change jobs, etc.

For those who want to get more sophisticated in creative dramatics, presentations may be given at increasing levels of complexity. Depending upon the vocational idea, the teacher chooses both the scope and sequence of the concept. For example, in an activity to increase job identification skills, the teacher asks a student to pantomime workers recently observed or discussed by the class. The other students guess the worker's job. At the next step of sophistication, appropriate music may be, "Truck Driver's Song" or "I've Been Working on the Railroad." At a third level of sophistication, exaggerated movement would next portray characteristics of job setting, i.e. in-doors, or out, carrying, or lifting, or driving. Class discussion then brings out characteristics of the portrayed job they found interesting and those they found uninteresting. The leader accepts all responses. The higher levels of sophistication in creative dramatics involve increasingly more dialogue and formality of presentation. Certain attitudes concerned with jobs can be presented at advanced levels such as dependability, punctuality, or cooperation.

PROPS: THE WORKER'S TOOLS

Props can be useful in getting across career concepts such as job safety, type of job, and understandings of job content. The teachers may want the students to focus upon specific work movements used with the props, for example, the grocery store cashier working the cash register. The students can build an assembly line and are asked to imagine the various sounds in the factory. Props can help illustrate a point or important concept such as cooperative efforts in getting jobs done or the extremely technical nature of equipment many workers are called upon to use. Numerous safety factors in the use of tools and work implements could also be emphasized by use of props. In creative dramatics there is neither a need nor a place for the sophisticated technical aids, such as lighting and scenery associated with drama and the theatre. Nor is there a place for a formal audience. The only desirable audience is that part of the creative dramatics group chosen to observe and enjoy a certain part of the playing (Siks, 1958).

Have fun!

REFERENCES

Cole, N. R. *The Arts in the Classroom*. New York: John Day, 1940.

Fitzgerald, B. *World Tales for Creative Dramatics and Storytelling*. New York: Prentice-Hall, 1962.

Kase, R. *Stories for Creative Acting*. New York: Samuel French, 1961.

Kerman, G. *Plays and Creative Ways with Children*. New York: Harvey House, 1961.

McCaslin, N. *Creative Dramatics in the Classroom*. New York: David McKay, 1968.

Mearns, H. *Creative Power*. New York: Dover Publications, 1958.

Siks, G. B. *Creative Dramatics, An Art for Children*. New York: Harper & Row, 1958.

Ward, W. *Playmaking with Children*. New York: Appleton-Century, 1957.

Woods, M. "Creative Teaching Tips," *Keeping Up with Elementary Education*, 1971, 16, 12–13.

Woods M. "Creative Teaching Tips," *Keeping Up with Elementary Education*, 1971, 17, 14–15.

Yawkey, T. & Aronin, G. "Communication Skills with Primary Grades," *Trust: Leadership for Education*, 1972.

PART VI
Exceptional Children

Introductory Comments

Teachers of exceptional children frequently use dramatization to focus on interaction and self-expression. Activities involving exceptional children are frequently individualized, and creative dramatics offer an approach to meet the needs of these special youngsters.

"Ms. Green's Garden" by Milton Reiling details his development of a play as a vehicle to integrate his classes in special education. The play itself is easy to stage, and directions for costumes, plus the script itself, are given.

Elaine Hoffman Wagener describes the use of dramatization to teach historical events, personalities, and feelings to a group of children with visual impairments. "Drama: Key to History for the Visually Impaired Child" shows that drama can incorporate body movement and intellectual content to strengthen these children's thinking skills.

Working with gifted and learning disabled students, Michael Rothstein, as described by Bryna Paston in "The Pied Piper's Magic Endures," uses theatrical experiences as a teaching tool. In an effort to combine the talents of the students of various achievement levels, he succeeds in teaching more than information.

ERIC materials have long provided resources for educators. Gail Cohen Taylor has compiled an annotated bibliography entitled "Creative Dramatics for Handicapped Children" which presents "information from and about ERIC materials that discuss various types of creative dramatics activities, outline the advantages of creative dramatics for handicapped children, and suggest techniques for using creative dramatics with children who are mentally, physically, or emotionally handicapped."

Ms. Green's Garden

by Milton Reiling

The first year I taught in an inner-city school, I had three classes composed of retarded, learning disabled and emotionally disturbed children. They were grouped together in a federally-funded program that attempted to eliminate the usual special education labels and, whenever possible, integrate these students socially and academically.

I quickly became frustrated by the students' lack of motivation and by the seemingly endless fighting that disrupted classroom activities. The children's problems were caused not only by a background of extreme poverty, but also by feelings of low self-esteem that often accompany placement in a special ed class. I didn't need a psychologist or social worker to tell me that little would be accomplished academically if I failed to motivate these children and help them realize their self-worth.

Before full success in the three R's of the academic world can be achieved, I feel that the three R's of socialization are necessary: respect, restraint and responsibility. These three R's must be taught on a daily basis through positive reinforcement and good role models; however, at the time I was looking for one major project which would enable me to begin development of these skills and also socially and academically integrate the three groups.

I began with the concept that almost all children enjoy playacting. Having listened to my students' daily conversations regarding TV, I suggested that they produce and star in their own show for the entire school. They were skeptical at first, but soon jumped in with great enthusiasm.

THE THREE R'S

Respect, the first of the three R's of socialization, is the trait most obviously nurtured by a drama project. A production engenders self-respect, requires children to respect and cooperate with each other and frequently earns the respect of older siblings and parents who are in the audience. Also, as a result of a successful production, "normal" children often show a marked change in attitude towards children in special education classes.

A theatrical production also requires students to practice restraint. The children found it much easier to work together since they had an exciting, important goal in common. They knew they could not waste time fighting; they had to perform in front of their peers. When arguments did erupt, rehearsal was stopped immediately. Later, when cooler heads prevailed, we would always discuss what would happen to the production if they could not restrain themselves from arguing and fighting.

Responsibility was necessary in order to have a successful play. Each child was responsible for his own part and, to some extent, his costume. The children quickly realized that if one person lagged behind in learning dialogue or dance movements, the play suffered. The children were made to understand that a successful production does not depend on talent alone; they also had sole responsibility for their own success.

The play, *Ms. Green's Garden*, not only helped improve the children's self-respect, but also brought about an atmosphere which facilitated a successful integration of the three classes. An added benefit was that the play served as a bridge between community and school; it provided a great opportunity for a positive visit by parents when they came to see their "stars" in action.

IDEAL VEHICLE

There are many features in this particular play which make it an ideal vehicle for special education children. For example, it's a simple play, with most of the characters having only one or two lines of dialogue. Longer dialogue contains many repetitious lines, making the parts relatively easy to learn. Since most of my children could not read, their lines were repeated to them each day until the parts were learned. Ad-libbing was never criticized; if anything, it was encouraged.

Also, the costumes are colorful, yet simple and inexpensive to make. Only a few props are needed. And with a few simple adjustments on teacher's part, the play can have as few as eight characters or as many as 30.

The action takes place in Ms. Green's garden. The following characters can be used: Ms. Green, four flowers (Iris, Petunia, Daisy and Rose), two weeds, a weeping willow tree, the sun, four dancing clouds, four bad guys and the good guy, Earthman. (Earthman can be dressed à la Superman, in the Earth Week colors of green and yellow.)

The clouds are cut from heavy cardboard and painted white, with light blue cleaning bags around the edges to give the effect of billowing clouds; the rain cloud is painted dark gray. Flowers can be made from posterboard, with holes in the center for each child's face. Corrugated paper, suitably painted, can be used for trees and weeds. It's a good idea, by the way, to let the children use their imagination in helping to make their costumes.

The play begins with Ms. Green working in her garden.

Ms. Green: Hello, don't you just love my beautiful plants? I think I'll water my plants. All plants need four things—air, water, soil and sunlight. (*She goes to each plant and waters it.*) Hello, Pansy. Hello, Iris. Hello, Daisy. Hello, Rose. (*Seeing the weeds, she yells in great alarm.*) Those darned old weeds. (*She takes the weeds by their ears and pulls them offstage. She then approaches the weeping willow, who begins to cry loudly.*)

Weeping Willow: Waa! Waa! (*Continues to cry, but not as loudly.*)

Ms. Green: That old weeping willow. All it ever does is cry. It's just like a cry-baby. (*She moves to center stage.*) I think I'll go to the store and get some food for my plants. It will make them even stronger. (*She exits and music—such as "Raindrops Keeping Falling on My Head" or "Forty-second Street"—begins. The first cloud enters, dances to center stage, then dances back and picks up a second cloud. This continues until all four clouds are center stage in front of the sun and plants. At the end of a simple dance routine—e.g., kick and step—each cloud sits on the floor and lays the cardboard prop down flat.*)

Cloud 1: We

Cloud 2: Are

Cloud 3: The

Cloud 4: CLOUDS.

Cloud 1: We bring rain.

Cloud 2: We help the flowers grow.

Cloud 3: We help the weeping willow grow.

Cloud 4: But today we are going to be bad. We're not going to let the sun get through to the plants. (*The clouds stand up and lift their cardboard props. Ms. Green enters.*)

Ms. Green: Oh, no! Oh, no! (*She slaps her forehead.*) What am I going to do? How can I get rid of these clouds? I'll have to blow them away. I'm going to need some help. Will the children in the front row help me blow them away? (*Ms. Green blows and clouds "float" offstage. The flowers and trees perk up immediately.*) Oh, good. Now my flowers are pretty again. They have the four things that they need in order to grow—air, water, sun and good soil. I think I'll go get some ice cream. (*As she says this, the four bad guys enter, dressed as villains out of a silent movie. The leader stops suddenly: the other three run into him and fall down. They scramble to their feet.*)

Bad Guy 1: Let's ruin Ms. Green's garden.

Bad Guy 2: Let's get rid of these pretty flowers.

Bad Guy 3: I don't like all these pretty flowers around here. They stink. (*He holds his nose.*)

Bad Guy 4: Let's get rid of that cry-baby, the Weeping Willow. (*The willow begins to cry loudly. Ms. Green moans, twirls around and faints as the bad guys run from flower to flower, causing each of the flowers to droop. The bad guys exit to the Dragnet theme. As they exit, Earthman enters. He "flies" around the stage, his arms outstretched and his cape billowing. With a short jump, he dramatically lands center stage. He then flexes his muscles.*)

Earthman: Earthman to the rescue. I've come to save the day. The plants need four things: air, soil, water and sunlight. I will make sure they get them. (*He stops in mid-turn and stage whispers to the audience.*) Remember, if you ever need help for your plants, call me. Credit cards accepted. (*He turns toward the flowers and yells.*) Never fear, I am here. (*The plants rejuvenate as Earthman flies around them. He then flies offstage, jumping over Ms. Green's body. Cloud 4—the dark gray cloud—dances onstage to music.*)

Cloud 4: Don't worry. I'll wake her up. (*The cloud leans over Ms. Green and sprinkles water—torn paper—over her and then swaggers offstage.*)

Ms. Green (*rising*): Oh, what happened? Where am I? Oh, now I remember. My poor plants. (*She turns away from the audience and sees that the plants are fine.*) They look better than ever. (*She then repeats the beginning of the play, going to the plants and trees, saying hello to them and watering them. The weeping willow begins to cry and Ms. Green goes to center stage.*) I am so happy that my plants have the four things they need to be healthy—sun, water, air and good soil. I'd like to pick a rose and give it to you for being such a good audience. (*Ms. Green goes over to the rose and walks the rose to center stage. The curtain closes.*)

Drama: Key to History for the Visually Impaired Child

by Elaine Hoffman Wagener

Concepts of history are often difficult for children to relate to in a concrete way. Dramatization of important historic events and personalities is an aid to the internalization of concepts and understandings in this area.

Children with visual impairments need a variety of stimuli to facilitate learning, as do all children. However, the use of the whole body in creative dramatics gives the visually impaired child the opportunity needed to gain control of his movements and to grow in his sense of personal space. It allows children the possibility of relating to each other in an exploration of the space shared by the other actors. Drama enables children to use their bodies as a primary tool and encourages them to move naturally and easily.

Most of the writing by authorities in children's dramatics and "play-making" has discouraged formalized dramas for children. Memorization of lines and movements, elaborate costumes constructed by eager mothers, and time-consuming rehearsals are not considered appropriate to the needs of children. "Getting the play ready" takes hours of instructional time which possibly could have been spent more profitably in other ways.

Nevertheless, teachers continue to have children memorize lines and spend hours perfecting the end result. Why? The rewards of the formal type of play-giving are apparent. The parents are pleased and proud to see their Johnny and Marcia on stage, in costume, reeling off the lines they have worked so hard to learn. The teachers can smile and take much of the credit for having produced this off-Broadway success. The children, like all actors, are thankful they made it through the final curtain. The final product is an ego-building experience and certainly is a positive feature.

However, the process to achieve the end product is not always as positive. Learning lines is an anxiety-producing activity for many children. Rehearsals become periods of friction and conflict when children are asked to sit quietly while others perform. Teachers, too, get tired and impatient and make remarks which are cutting and degrade the child's abilities. Whatever meaning was inherent in the materials when the play was fresh is lost to the children long before the play ever reaches its "polished" form.

How, then, can we dramatize special events in history in a way which will be a positive educational experience for the children we teach?

One way is to focus on the *content* of history rather than on the *form* of the drama. For example, if the area to be studied is early American history, we would try to excite children with the adventure of those early events, to expose children to the real people of those days and to recapture the flavor of that period. Teachers could read short biographies or excerpts from historic novels if they were not available in braille. Other sources of information could be guest speakers, records, films, and television pro- grams. If reference books are not available in braille, the teacher or interested parents could tape important information on cassettes to be played by the children individually or in small groups. If the information needed is available in braille, an older child could assist in recording the material on tapes. Visits to local historical sites should not be overlooked in working with children who are visually impaired. This enrichment of their background and the sensory stimulation will help their history "come alive."

Children might choose one important person of the times—John Adams, Betsy Ross, Crispus Attucks, Benjamin Franklin—and learn enough about that period to "become" him or her. Small groups could be formed to study some of the happenings—The Boston Tea Party; the Boston Massacre; battles at Lexington, Concord and Bunker Hill; the Tea and Stamp Act; the Consitutional Convention.

Then, as an outgrowth of this study, several types of dramatizations might occur either with or without an audience of class members.

A television talk show could be an impromptu activity in which the teacher or a student could be host and interview people of the period— Ethan Allen, Paul Revere, John Paul Jones, or Thomas Payne.

Situational drama could also take place with one child describing a situation and the characters and class members volunteering to "role- play." An example of a situation: "You are a colonist, and your neighbor rides over to talk to you about the events of the times. He believes it is disloyal to fight England. You try to convince him that he is wrong. You might talk to him about the Stamp Act and other grievances." Another situation might be this: "You are soldiers at Breed's Hill. The British have charged the Hill twice already. Colonel William Prescott has just talked to you, encouraging you to be brave and remember why you are fighting. You are out of powder and are discussing among yourselves the possibility of getting more from the troops at Bunker Hill.'' Situations like these could be brailled on cards and chosen randomly from a file by the children.

Other outgrowths of immersion in the period could occur in ''plays'' in which each small group gets together and decides how to depict the information they have gathered.

The teacher's role in spontaneous ''playing'' is crucial. Instead of prompting by saying the line the child has forgotten and having the child repeat it, as in the case where a script has been memorized, the teacher assumes a questioning role. She might ask, ''What would George Washington likely have said when his troops were trapped behind British lines? How would he have felt?' or ''How does that make you feel to know you have to pay taxes to a government which will not allow you to vote?'' Other questions based on the feelings of the characters and the mood of the event will help draw out the children's responses.

Sometimes children who are handicapped in the use of one of their senses become deficient in the development of their abstract and symbolic thinking. It is hoped that some of this possible deficiency can be partially ameliorated by creating a learning environment rich in sensory stimuli. The use of informal drama is one avenue to an enriched curriculum. Through it children may become more secure in their own capabilities, their use of language, and their power over their own bodies. They also will be strengthening their thinking skills as well as growing in their understanding of history.

The Pied Piper's Magic Endures

by Bryna Paston

In a suburban Philadelphia school 20 sixth graders are savoring the after-glow of a hit. The run is over, the reviews are raves, and now they're remembering more than the moments onstage—a whole year of learning, planning, improvising, and rehearsing.

"I'd have to be honest and say I was nervous about the whole thing," admits Matt. The 20 youngsters are sitting in a circle. "But I've discovered that we're all kids."

"I found out it was okay if I made mistakes," says Bobby. "At first I worried a lot about that. Especially the teasing I might get."

"Here," says Carol, "almost no one teases us."

"Some kids in the school still tease us, though," Bobby reminds her. "Oh, sometimes they call us slow, sometimes even weird."

Peggy speaks up, "Some kids don't associate with us because they say we're eggheads."

"It helped to have Obie in the play," says Steve. (Obie, a main character in *The Pied Piper*, is crippled.)

"Because Obie was different from the other children in the town," says Lisa, "they teased him. He was lonely. He wanted to be able to run and dance. But more than anything, Obie wanted to be accepted by the other children."

"Obie," says Ted, "is a lot like us."

The 20 sixth graders divide equally between learning disabled and gifted students. Bobby, Carol, and Steve spend part of the time in a regular classroom at Round Meadow Elementary School in Pennsylvania's Upper Moreland School District and, depending on each one's needs, are also receiving special education. Matt, Peggy, and Lisa are in the school's gifted program. Last year, they and the rest of the 20 sixth graders produced a two-act play, *The Pied Piper*. How they grew to feel comfortable and candid with one another is a story in itself.

The whole idea began as two separate thoughts in one teacher's mind. For two years, Michael Rothstein had watched the learning disabled students in the Round Meadow school cafeteria sitting off to themselves at a corner table. Being in regular classrooms did not seem to change the youngsters' social isolation.

Rothstein was also thinking about how to challenge his class of gifted children with whom he'd been working for three years. Although Rothstein and the youngsters had done many creative projects together, he worried that if they were to become leaders, they should be getting to know other youngsters better than they had. He also worried that they considered themselves to be too perfect.

Why not, thought Rothstein, challenge his gifted students by having them work with learning disabled students and, at the same time, help bring the learning disabled out of their social isolation? Rothstein recalled how his gifted group had taken to *The Wiz* (based on *The Wizard of Oz*) during a field trip to Philadelphia last term, particularly the feat of reshaping a classic.

Using theatrical experiences as a teaching tool is a natural technique for Rothstein, who has done this throughout his 17 years as classroom teacher and crisis counselor.

But Rothstein wanted to avoid the easy cliché of gifted kids tutoring the learning disabled. Rothstein suspected that each group had help for the other. "My gifted youngsters, if anything, were overconfident. They needed to discover that handicapped youngsters have leadership qualities, too. On the other hand, LD youngsters fear criticism and shun leadership roles."

As a child, Rothstein had his share of adjustment to school and he got some help from teachers along the way. Back in Trenton, New Jersey, in the 1940s, his fifth grade teacher Lois Tobish was a stern schoolmarm with rigid standards. "But her kids," says Rothstein, "knew she cared. Even the ones from poor homes. She'd come in with dresses that she told us she'd bought for her niece. Mumbling something about the dresses not fitting her niece, she'd give them to different girls in the class. Years later, I realized she didn't have a niece.

"I used to beg my father for a crewcut so Miss Tobish couldn't grab my hair. You know, she was the only teacher who ever whacked me with a ruler, but she was also the only one who ever hugged me."

He also remembers his eighth grade history teacher Bill Carnigan. Hating school, Rothstein often played truant, taking out a boat on the Delaware River—as he says, "to read stories I liked, not school stuff. But," says Rothstein, "Carnigan had a way of filling his classes with juicy tidbits about the doings of kings and queens, much like a soapie that is continued tomorrow. It got so I had to keep coming back to find out what happened.

"Anyway, I owed him 15 written assignments and I wasn't doing anything about them. Some kids stole my private notebooks of poems and stories and showed them to Carnigan. He told me to write a book report on my own work and that would count for all 15 assignments. It was an offer I couldn't refuse.

"He made me see myself as a writer and as someone who is competent. It made quite a difference to me. I started coming regularly to school and doing well in classes. Four kids from that history class became teachers because of Bill Carnigan." One of the youngsters, of course, was Rothstein.

For Rothstein, now fortyish and settled in at Round Meadow, ideas like mixing gifted and LD students come naturally. The real challenge is to do them. Rothstein sought out Beverly Sigafoos, special education teacher for the school district, then teaching a class of learning disabled sixth graders at Round Meadow. She warmed to the idea, volunteering her help. One firm rule they agreed upon: *no script*. A learning disabled youngster generally has trouble with reading, and a script would be too threatening. "We hatched a way around that by having one of us write down the dialog as the youngsters improvised. When they forgot a line, we fed it to them. We also used a tape recorder and videotape. Being able to see and hear their performances caught the youngsters' fancy so that mistakes became less important."

Once the principal approved the project, Rothstein approached his gifted students. "They reacted enthusiastically," he remembers, "particularly with *The Wiz* fresh in their minds."

He went down to Sigafoos's class and explained the play and what they would be doing—improvising a script based on a legend, and then acting out and producing the show. "We talked," says Rothstein, "about the characters." He found the youngsters less than lukewarm to the idea. "I couldn't seem to bring them out, get them to talk beyond the usual polite yes or no," says Rothstein, who usually has a knack for putting youngsters at ease. "I didn't know enough then to realize they were full of fears, self-doubts about performing and goofing up lines and risking ridicule from the gifted students, whom they didn't know."

It wasn't easy to get Sigafoos's students to attend the first joint meeting. "We practically had to push them there," says Rothstein. To break the ice, he asked each student to make name tags that gave more than just the name. "I suggested they give a hint about themselves, tell something on the tag that they might want people to know," explains Rothstein. "Well, they tried, but most didn't get beyond their names."

What surprised Rothstein more than anything was the reserve of his own gifted students. He had been counting on them to open up Sigafoos's youngsters. But no. They hung back awkwardly and volunteered nothing. The two groups sat on opposite sides of the room and stared uncomfortably. "Instead of a group, we had Beverly's group and mine. And somehow we had thought that the two groups would hit it off instantly."

Not one to be discouraged, Rothstein held a second meeting. He subdivided the youngsters into random groups of three or four, mixing gifted with learning disabled. "For the moment we forgot about the play and turned to improvisation," he says. "I asked each subgroup to 'be' a piece of equipment—in 60 seconds or less. Bobby, one of the learning disabled students, caught the idea immediately and inspired his group to become a pinball machine. The skit drew warm applause from the group. It was a breakthrough. A learning disabled student had picked up the ball as group leader."

It was time to turn to the play. "I eased them into it, talking about how a play is built around a problem and then the search for a solution," explains Rothstein. "We did some research on the Pied Piper legend. The students discovered that a town called Hamelin really does exist in West Germany, and the legend is believed to have grown out of an actual incident sometime in the 13th century. They also found that poets and storytellers sometimes draw upon a classic like the Pied Piper—as did Goethe, Robert Browning, and the brothers Grimm.

"We pieced out the basic legend. A magician, the Pied Piper, appears one day in the town of Hamelin, and for a fee, agrees to rid the town of rats. He keeps his promise by playing a flute and luring the rats into the Weser River. When the town reneges on its promise to pay him, he also charms away the children."

With the storyline clearly in mind, Rothstein turned to casting. Each weekly session of several hours was built around one main character, particularly mannerisms, feelings, and phrasing. Everyone who wanted to try out for the character would then take a turn auditioning. "We started with Obie's mother," recalls Rothstein, "how hard her life had been and how she was strong because of this. The youngsters admired her.

"To ease the way, Beverly and I got up in the middle of the circle and did some impromptu dialog. Then various youngsters auditioned as the mother. We never hurried anyone. If someone was partway through and wanted to start over, we let them. In fact, we hadn't even set dates for the performances. We wanted them to take their time."

Neither Rothstein nor Sigafoos did the casting. Instead, the group voted. To spread the lead roles around, Rothstein double-cast. One youngster might be the Pied Piper one evening and a town resident the next. With six performances, each cast would appear three times in a role. Without anyone intending it, the leads were split between gifted and LD students.

Julie, a learning disabled student with dyslexia, expressed a wish to try out for the mother's part. But she would not ask to audition. "I knew she wanted the part," says Rothstein, "but she was terrified of getting up to audition. She didn't really trust the group. Finally one youngster said to Julie, 'I was so sure when I got up there that nothing would come out. But it did. You'll see. Go on and try. If you're stuck, we'll help you. We'll give you the words.'

"Julie got up," Rothstein continues. "Taking a breadbasket for a prop, she approached the youngster playing Obie as he sat alone on the stage. She knelt down and said, 'Didn't I hear children here?' He nodded. Putting her arm around Obie, Julie whispered, 'Were they teasing you?' "

Rothstein looked over and saw that Ted, a youngster who is seldom still, was glued to his chair and listening intently. "Nobody made a sound," he recalls. "Julie got the part. I must add, however, that she didn't learn her songs. I decided to let the situation go. But during one rehearsal, she got up there, opened her mouth to sing, and nothing came out. She was embarrassed into going home that evening and learning all three songs for the next rehearsal."

With Rothstein's encouragement, the youngsters made some changes in their version of the Pied Piper legend. They had one of the town children who had been teasing Obie in the first scene show sympathy for the boy. Further, they decided to bestow upon the piper human emotions, particularly anger at the mayor's refusal to pay as promised. The group saw the piper in more human than mythical terms.

As a gesture to women's equality, it was decided to create the character of Katrina, a vegetable vender who leads the women into pressuring the mayor and his two aldermen to act on the rat problem. Later, when the mayor has messed things up by refusing to pay the piper, Katrina is compassionate, telling the mayor he has done some good things too. Government, the youngsters concluded, means working things out. They felt the mayor was the wiser for his mistakes.

Throughout the rehearsals, if anyone was having trouble with a part, the group would return to games or exercises. "We'd just stop," says Rothstein. "Maybe we'd do trust activities. I might ask, Whom do you trust in the group enough to fall backward against? or Who are the characters in the play who really trust each other? Who are the ones who don't?"

After a nervous couple of months, friendships began to form. Julie and one of the gifted students, for instance, became pals. Rothstein's gifted students took to going down to the LD classroom to try out the air hockey game. "I could really feel they were accepting one another," says Rothstein, ''when that single table of learning disabled students in the school cafeteria became two tables pushed together so cast members could work on the play while they ate lunch.''

The only formality connected with the play was a run-of-the-play contract specifying that each performer and crew member be on time, give and take positive criticism, and respect others' opinions. The idea of spelling out their responsibilities appealed to the youngsters. On the day the contracts were signed, Rothstein recalls, each youngster brought along a trusted friend to witness the agreements and also sign the paper. The youngsters even suggested that Rothstein and Sigafoos draw up contracts, which both did.

As the play progressed, so did the youngsters. There was Ted who has a non-retentive memory. With the others learning lines quickly, those on stage with Ted had to listen to every word he said because it always came out differently. All the same, he was never at a loss for words and his fellow performers learned to accommodate themselves to his non-retentive memory.

Ted also had trouble remembering the words to his songs. A parent watching one rehearsal suggested writing the lyrics on a menu that Ted held in one scene. Once Ted had the words on the menu, he never needed to look at them. Just knowing the words were there was enough.

There was an unplanned addition to the crew. ''We had a fifth grader—neither gifted nor learning disabled—who came to every rehearsal,'' says Rothstein. ''He desperately wanted to be in the play, to be involved.'' Rothstein invited him to work with the group. ''I put him in charge of the lights and he was terrific,'' says Rothstein. ''The group voted him an associate member for the rest of the year.''

Parents had a way of coming for a session and staying, getting involved. A mother volunteered to play the piano. A former professional dancer, a friend of Rothstein's who has her own dance group, donated her time. She did all the choreography. Many others gave hours of their time to sew costumes and help build sets.

When the final evening performance played to a capacity crowd of 350 last June, the parents, teachers, and community loved it. The question Rothstein heard the most that evening was, Which are the LD children and which are the gifted?

Creative Dramatics for Handicapped Children

by Gail Cohen Taylor

Noreen. When I listen to my tapes of the early [creative dramatics] sessions, it is very difficult to identify Noreen. Quiet, unassertive, somewhat withdrawn, she seemed always overwhelmed by the more aggressive children. She was always attentive but never chose an active role for herself. Her initial participation was always tentative. It was not until we were well into our final improvisation that I noticed a change. The concept of *The Last Tree* seemed to affect her strongly. She wrote a beautiful story about *The Last Tree*. . . . When her team decided to be "the bad guys" who were going to destroy the *Tree* Noreen flatly refused to do it . . . even in fun. No one could persuade her that it was only make-believe. . . . As rehearsals progressed, I noticed that she had chosen one line to say and invariably said it loud and clear and seemed to relish her moment. At one rehearsal, the "interviewer" (one of the characters) . . . left the rehearsal early and, desperate for a run-through, I asked Noreen if she could possible take his place. She went through the whole opening scene almost "word-perfect" (proving just how attentive she had been!) and earned herself an ovation from the rest of the class. Consequently I changed the opening sequence and for the final performance Noreen shared the "interviewing" and came through beautifully.

—Teacher's account, reported in *A Theatre
Workshop for Children with Learning Disabilities*,
by Lotte Kaliski [ED 158 541, p. 16–17]

This description illustrates many of the benefits that creative dramatics offers children with learning disabilities and other handicaps: active participation in a group effort, growth of self-confidence, development of listening and speaking skills, and carry-over to other language arts areas such as composition. Of course, creative dramatics has positive values for all children, as many teachers have discovered; but it has been found especially helpful in promoting the development of children with many kinds of handicaps. This article will present information from and about

ERIC materials that discuss various types of creative dramatics activities, outline the advantages of creative dramatics for handicapped children, and suggest techniques for using creative dramatics with children who are mentally, physically, or emotionally handicapped.

TYPES OF CREATIVE DRAMATICS ACTIVITIES

As noted in "Creative Dramatics" [ED 154 547], the term creative dramatics implies activities without formal or strict guidelines: the focus is on self-expression and cooperative interaction and on the process rather than the product. Creative dramatics encompasses a wide variety of activities, including rhythmic movement and dance, sensory awareness exercises, pantomime, improvisation, role playing, acting out stories, and developing original, scripted plays. Since the emphasis is on children's development, activities may be adapted freely to meet the needs of individual children, as illustrated by the script changes made by Noreen's teacher in the account cited previously.

Creative Dramatics in the Elementary School [ED 154 434], which presents detailed suggestions for conducting creative dramatics activities, notes that "because creative dramatics is totally adjustable to any group, the principles and methods discussed throughout this handbook are readily applicable to special education classes. The use of creative dramatics with a special education class, as with any group, depends first on the teacher's knowledge of students and their levels of development." (p. 5).

Duke [ED 096 673] outlines a sequence for creative dramatics activities that begins with work in rhythm and movement and continues with mime and pantomime, improvisation, role playing, and finally the development of scripted plays.

ADVANTAGES OF CREATIVE DRAMATICS FOR HANDICAPPED CHILDREN

Rosenthal [ED 157 847] observes that the arts (including music, movement, visual arts, and drama) can help reveal the latent creative talents of handicapped children and promote their development. Kaliski [ED 158 541] similarly notes that drama taps resources in learning disabled children that very often have been unknown to teachers; she discusses many therapeutic effects of drama, including the alleviation of deficiencies in body image, coordination, time and space orientation, thought sequencing, and visual, auditory, and tactile perception. She concludes that perhaps the most important aspect of drama activities is their beneficial effect on the learning disabled child's emotional and social growth.

Observing that all handicapped children are in some way alienated from their environment and isolated from normal social growth experiences, Schattner [ED 011 428] points out that the arts can help such children clarify their concepts about reality, come into closer contact with each other, and gain insight into social relationships.

Creative Dramatics in the Elementary School [ED 154 434] points out that creative dramatics fosters a positive self-image in special education students, since every idea is acceptable, and there are no wrong answers. Many other writers also stress the fact that there are no right or wrong answers in creative dramatics and reflect on the advantages this has for children who feel inadequate in academic subjects.

Creative dramatics frequently has a positive effect on language development. Duke [ED 096 673] observes that dramatic play—as a natural, flexible activity with speech as its core—stimulates language, provides motivation for children with speech disabilities to improve their speech, and improves the articulation skills of some children. Schattner [ED 011 428] reflects that when children are encouraged to use their own language in creating play dialogue, they gain an understanding of language as a means of communication and develop a feel and respect for it.

Ehrlich [ED 105 464] finds that when children with speech disabilities are given many opportunities to communicate through pantomime, they develop feelings of security as they are accepted by the group and will eventually attempt to speak more frequently. She also points out that drama helps children develop the use of nonverbal communication to express themselves in ways their limited vocabularies would otherwise prohibit.

CREATIVE DRAMATICS FOR MENTALLY HANDICAPPED CHILDREN

Jennings [ED 113 715], a creative drama resource teacher, reports her dismay at so often being asked to work with bright groups since—in the view of many teachers—"the others would be hopeless at it" (p. 36). She observes that, if it is a question of choice, the slow-learning groups should in fact have priority; and she notes that, contrary to the common misconception, low-ability children often have fewer preconceived ideas of what they "should" do than high-ability children, and they therefore produce more original and unconventional drama. Jennings provides guidelines for working with mentally handicapped students and describes activities that involved a class of retarded boys in building improvisations on Western and sailor themes.

Ehrlich [ED 105 464] notes the value of sense memory exercises for mentally handicapped children, finding that they help such children develop an awareness of their surroundings, distinguish individual parts of their environment, develop perceptually, and increase their vocabularies. She describes many sense memory exercises, including pretending to play with ice, wear an itchy sweater, eat a piece of fruit (while others try to guess which kind it is), and peel and smell an onion. She cautions that material for mentally handicapped children should be simple and should deal with familiar topics, and that dialogue will have to be minimal and may have to be prompted or provided by the teacher.

"Creative Dramatics" [ED 154 547] offers suggestions for using such pantomime activities as pretending to be mirrors (reflecting motions and expressions of the leader or a partner), spaceships blasting off, and cooked and uncooked spaghetti; it also stresses the need for drawing on familiar experiences when working with low functioning children. It suggests that as individuals become less inhibited, half the group can serve as an audience and half as performers, with individuals eventually performing alone.

A summer creative movement and dance program for trainable mentally retarded children is described by Crumbliss and Wenger [ED 157 343]. They discuss the activities used, noting that much repetition of basic concepts was provided; report on the dramatic increases that were seen in children's rhythmic ability; tell of the participants' increasing pleasure in successful communication and self-expression; and observe that the emphasis on rhythmic movement helped the children's speech directly by demonstrating the cadence and phrasing of words and sentences.

In an article in *Arts for the Handicapped Child. Why?* [ED 161 214], Amy Zehm reports the remarkable effects of musical and dramatic activities on "Pam," an educable mentally handicapped child who, although she had the least mental ability of any child in the class, learned songs quickly and retained them. A series of songs, accompanied by action games, was used to teach her to recognize and name colors and to learn other basic skills and concepts. The group also did a great deal of singing, folk dancing, play acting, and production of puppet shows. Zehm tells that at the start of the program Pam "made her wants known with pointing and one-word commands. She was untrained, unkempt, and unhappy. Today [two and one-half years later] she is a neat, happy, extremely verbal, well-mannered little girl. She knows all her color words by sight and has completed the first pre-primer and started the second. . . . She can count and write to one hundred, do addition and subtraction problems to ten with pictures . . . expresses herself in complete sentences, dances simple folk dances, and knows literally hundreds of songs by heart." (p. 41).

CREATIVE DRAMATICS FOR PHYSICALLY HANDICAPPED CHILDREN

Jennings [ED 113 715] provides guidelines for working with blind and deaf children and with children in wheelchairs, and she observes the valuable contribution of drama in taking the focus off children's physical handicaps. She notes that children have been known to attempt completely new movements spontaneously while absorbed in an exciting theme, citing the case of a child who stood for the first time during a mime game. Schattner [ED 011 428] also describes methods for working with children with various physical handicaps and shows how to help children in wheelchairs perform "wheelchair dances."

Gamble [ED 136 516] reports on a creative drama program for severely physically handicapped secondary students; the activities described could also be used with elementary students. Gamble's students participated in sensory awareness activities, pantomimes, and movement to music and then developed plots for stories that were made into radio dramas and tape recorded.

Rosenthal [ED 157 847] urges teachers to "be willing to take kids out of wheelchairs [for drama activities]. Respect their hesitancy, but be encouraging. As much direct contact as possible with their environment is stimulating and productive of self-esteem." (p. 8).

CREATIVE DRAMATICS FOR EMOTIONALLY DISTURBED CHILDREN

A creative dramatics program for a group of eight emotionally disturbed children is described by Gillies [ED 091 771]. The group began with pantomime, which Gillies feels makes acting fluid and close to real life before the complication of dialogue is introduced. Other activities included experiences with sound and touch, making up a group plot for a play, and working in pairs to plan out the play scene-by-scene, with the teacher eventually writing down the dialogue. Gillies found that the group created situations in their play that related to their own problems and that, through exploring the feelings of their characters, they gained in self-understanding.

Ehrlich [ED 105 464] points out that creative dramatics is beneficial for emotionally disturbed children, both those who are hyperactive and those who are withdrawn, since the teacher encourages freedom within a set of limits. She warns, however, that individuals who are not trained as therapists should not attempt to do psychodrama with disturbed children. Jennings [ED 113 715] issues a similar warning but does point to techniques developed through psychodrama that can be incorporated, with care, into remedial situations. She provides general guidelines for working with disturbed children and includes practical illustrations of drama activities used with groups of such children.

CREATIVE DRAMATICS FOR CHILDREN WITH OTHER DISABILITIES

Gillies [ED 091 771] describes the creative dramatics activities she used with a group of brain injured children who demonstrated limited language development and puzzling, erratic behavior. She tells how she first enabled the children to learn the meaning of listening and of quiet, and she includes transcripts of class sessions to show how she used creative dramatics activities that stimulated all the senses; assisted children to think clearly and sequentially and to remember what had been said; helped them hear and gain respect for their own ideas; and encouraged them in building their own language, both verbal and nonverbal. Gillies observed a growing facility with language among the children and also noticed that some severe speech blocking and repetitions in several of the children all but disappeared during the program.

Duke [ED 096 673] tells how creative drama can foster improved speech performance in children with speech disabilities and describes types of ear and sound training that can be beneficial.

Telling how actors conducted a drama program at a school for children with learning disabilities, Kaliski [ED 158 541] describes how the program progressed from body movement exercises, pantomime, exploration of shapes, and a series of improvised short plays to the development of a play based on a theme provided by the actor-teachers. She tells how the children's play script grew out of their descriptions of characters and points to the great improvement in oral expression skills that resulted. Kaliski presents comments about the program by the actor-teachers and the children, and she includes several case studies that show the positive effects of the program on individual students.

ADDITIONAL RESOURCES

Many of the materials mentioned in this article suggest other resources to aid the use of creative dramatics with handicapped children. Specifically, Schattner [ED 011 428] lists suggested phonograph records, music books, and song books; Gillies [ED 091 771] lists and annotates twenty resources for creative dramatics; and Duke [ED 096 673] provides a selected bibliography of publications about creative dramatics, as well as annotated lists of such resources as recommended readings for creative dramatics teachers, films useful as creative drama starters, and films for preservice and inservice training in creative drama.

In addition, *Materials on Creative Arts (Arts, Crafts, Dance, Drama, Music, Bibliotherapy) for Persons with Handicapping Conditions* [ED 158 857] lists more than 1,000 print resources that deal with creative arts for handicapped persons. The resources are divided into six subcategories, including general; dance, movement, and dance therapy; drama, psycho-drama, and puppetry; and music and music therapy. Audiovisual materials, pertinent organizations, and suppliers of materials and equipment are also listed.

The ERIC materials referred to above are only a few of those in the ERIC system that deal with handicapped children and creative dramatics. For further information on these topics, teachers may consult the monthly issues of *Resources in Education (RIE)* and *Current Index to Journals in Education (CIJE)* under such subject headings as "Creative Dramatics," "Drama," and "Handicapped Children."

REFERENCES

Arts for the Handicapped Child. Why? Washington, D.C.: National Committee, Arts for the Handicapped, 1978. [ED 161 214; EDRS Price: MF $0.83, PC $4.82 plus postage; also available from National Committee, Arts for the Handicapped, 1701 K Street, N.W., Suite 805, Washington, D.C. 20006. $2.50, $2.25 each for 10 or more, prepaid, 59pp.]

"Creative Dramatics." Washington, D.C.: American Alliance for Health, Physical Education, and Recreation, 1977. [ED 154 547; EDRS Price: MF $0.83 plus postage, PC not available from EDRS; available from American Alliance for Health, Physical Education, and Recreation, 1201 16th Street, N.W., Washington, D.C. 20036, $2.00, 9pp.]

Creative Dramatics in the Elementary School. Austin, Texas: Texas Education Agency, Austin Division of Curriculum Development, 1978. [ED 154 434; EDRS price: MF $0.83, PC $6.32 plus postage, 78pp.]

Crumbliss, Karen and Wenger, Lee. "Creative Movement for Retarded Children." Paper presented at the World Congress on Future Special Education. Stirling, Scotland, June 25–July 1, 1978. [ED 157 343; EDRS price: MF $0.83, PC $1.82 plus postage, 8pp.]

Duke, Charles R. *Creative Dramatics and English Teaching.* Urbana, Illinois: National Council of Teachers of English, 1974. [ED 096 673; not available from EDRS; available from National Council of Teachers of English, 1111 Kenyon Road, Urbana, Illinois 61801—Stock No. 08938; members $3.75, nonmembers, $4.95, 180pp.]

Ehrlich, Harriet W., ed. *Creative Dramatics Handbook. Revised Edition.* Philadelphia: Philadelphia School District, Office of Early Childhood Programs, 1974. [ED 105 464; EDRS Price: MF $0.83, PC $10.82 plus postage; also available from National Council of Teachers of English, 1111 Kenyon Road, Urbana, Illinois 61801—Stock No. 08970; members $5.00; nonmembers $6.95, 165pp.]

Gamble, Michael W. "A Pilot Program in Creative Growth for Severely Physically Handicapped Secondary Students of the Human Resources School, Albertson, New York: A Descriptive Study." 1977. [ED 136 516; EDRS Price: MF $0.83, PC $1.82 plus postage, 17pp.]

Gillies, Emily. *Creative Dramatics for All Children.* Washington, D.C.: Association for Childhood Education International, 1973. [ED 091 771; EDRS Price; MF $0.83 plus postage, PC not available from EDRS; available from Association for Childhood Education International, 3615 Wisconsin Avenue, N.W., Washington, D.C. 20016, $3.25, prepay orders less than $5.00, 53pp.]

Jennings, Sue. *Remedial Drama: A Handbook for Teachers and Therapists.* New York: Theatre Arts Books, 1974. [ED 113 715; not available from EDRS; available from Theatre Arts Books, 333 Sixth Avenue, New York, New York 10014, $7.45 cloth, 114pp.]

Kaliski, Lotte. "A Theatre Workshop for Children with Learning Disabilities." Paper presented at the World Congress on Future Special Education, Stirling, Scotland, June 25–July 1, 1978. [ED 158 541; EDRS price: MF $0.83, PC $1.82 plus postage, 22pp.]

Materials on Creative Arts (Arts, Crafts, Dance, Drama, Music, Bibliotherapy) for Persons with Handicapping Conditions. Revised. Washington, D.C.: American Alliance for Health, Physical Education, and Recreation, 1977. [ED 159 857; EDRS price: MF $0.83 plus postage, PC not available from EDRS; available from American Alliance for Health, Physical Education, and Recreation, 1201 16th Street, N.W., Washington, D.C. 20036, $4.00, 103pp.]

Rosenthal, Judy Sirota, ed. *Ideas for Kids: A Multi-Arts Approach to Fostering Creativity.* New Haven, Connecticut: Project SEARCH, a program of Area Cooperative Educational Services, 1978 [ED 157 847; EDRS Price: MF $0.83 plus postage, PC not available from EDRS, 132pp.]

Schattner, Regina. *Creative Dramatics for Handicapped Children.* New York: John Day Company, 1967. [ED 011 428; not available from EDRS, 160pp.]

PART VII
Libraries

Introductory Comments

Dramatization easily blends itself into the story hour of a library program, or it can also serve as the starting point for expanded activities. The library provides an environment which should already represent a place for sharing stories and storytelling; therefore, the transition into creative dramatics should be a smooth one.

Carole C. Huggins has extensive experience in drama and shares the expertise which she used in helping to develop a program of creative dramatics in a Virginia public library. In ''Creative Dramatics: A New Kind of Library Program,'' she describes the planning and development of the dramatization program, as well as its many benefits.

Often, dramatization is incorporated into the school media program. ''The Media Specialist and Dramatic Productions'' defines the media specialist's role as ranging from official researcher to writer of scripts. Celestine Bloomfield also offers numerous suggestions to help the media specialist who is responsible for a program or play.

Sarah Yoder Scott, in ''Not on Every Bush,'' presents an actual account of her class presentation of *Stone Soup* and discusses the way her class used the library for research. Scott's step-by-step recipe for those who wish to experiment with dramatization serves as a stimulus to encourage others to try it.

Creative Dramatics: A New Kind of Library Program

by Carole C. Huggins

What is creative dramatics? What does it take to start a creative dramatics program in a library? Why are children's librarians beginning to have creative dramatics programs? My experiences at the Duncan Branch of the Alexandria Library can, I think, answer some of these questions.

As a patron of the library I often observed from posters and handouts that the children's librarian, Mrs. Stella Reed, was developing various drama activities for the juvenile patrons of the library. I had worked with children in drama programs previously and was interested in finding an outlet for my interest. I approached Mrs. Reed with the idea of beginning creative dramatics classes at the library. She was unfamiliar with creative dramatics but was glad to learn new approaches and was appreciative for my help. Together Stella and I began an education process—she was to teach me much about libraries; I was to teach her about creative dramatics and its potential in libraries; together we would win mothers and children to creative dramatics and indirectly to the library.

It is difficult to explain quickly and concisely just what creative dramatics is. Certainly there have been numerous attempts to define creative dramatics in the literature on the subject over the last forty years or so. As with any experimental technique, many people have different views on the subject and are in favor of various approaches. But most are agreed on the basics. Creative dramatics is informal dramatic play for children. It is drama without the confines of a script. It may include, and usually does, a number of creative exercises including pantomime, rhythm, rhyme, improvisation, and story dramatization. No parts are permanently assigned in creative dramatics. The children take turns playing the various roles in their improvised plays.

The emphasis in creative dramatics is on cooperation, not competition. It is often said that in creative dramatics the child, not the play, is the thing. Most advocates of creative dramatics feel that it is unwise to put young children into formal plays. They feel that a better introduction to drama is a more informal one where the children are exposed to the essence of the drama (plot, dialogue, characterization, etc.) rather than forced to memorize lines and come out sounding like robots.

Creative dramatics has been and can be used in many different circumstances. It is used in the schools as a teaching tool particularly in language arts and the social sciences. Museums employ creative dramatics techniques in tours for children. Recreation departments and even religious groups support creative dramatics programs. In each circumstance the emphasis in the program is slightly different.

Because the emphasis of creative dramatics in the libraries is and should be related to books, sessions most usually are related to a story or a poem. Considered this way, creative dramatics seems a natural extension of story hour—a juvenile program many libraries have. (Of the forty-seven libraries responding to the PLSC/JMRT/VLA* Survey on Children's Programs in Public Libraries in Virginia and the Greater Washington Area, forty-four have story hour programs.) Because of this logical relationship, we decided to structure our initial creative dramatics class around the program already established, the story hour. The Duncan Branch of the Alexandria Library has had a story hour for pre-school children for some time. Creative dramatics seemed a logical outgrowth of story hour; the graduates of story hour could go on to creative dramatics.

We decided to offer creative dramatics to children ages 5–7 for three reasons: (1) the children were easy to reach through the Story Hour structure already established; (2) this group of children had mothers who were interested in and would support programs for their children at the library; and (3) older children at the library were already involved in a play presentation group at the library directed by Mrs. Reed.

Parental response too was good. Parents are always curious about what creative dramatics is and what their children are doing. I believe it is best to keep mothers from watching and possibly inhibiting the children when they are being introduced to creative dramatics. For this reason I usually ask the mothers to wait outside in the library, but I promise them a demonstration at the end of the sessions. I am always available after class to answer questions. Contact with the parents is essential to keep the program going. Mrs. Reed and I spend quite a bit of time contacting mothers through

*Report on the PLSC/JMRT/VLA Survey on Children's Programs in Public Libraries in Virginia and in the Greater Washington Area, Winter, 1973.

the mail and by telephone, reminding them of the meetings, and talking with them about their feelings about the sessions. Their input was often most useful and I learned a great deal in this way.

A pertinent question here is, why are libraries getting into creative dramatics. The answer relates to the reason why libraries are increasing their special programs. More and more we find people working in libraries who are multi-media-minded. They are interested in activities to stimulate circulation, but they are also interested in just bringing people into the library. "They believe that the provision of programs for children is a legitimate library activity in its own right and that a head count of juvenile attendance at juvenile library programs is almost as important a statistic as juvenile book circulation figures."*

In light of this, I make the case that creative dramatics is a particularly good and very practical program to institute. Creative dramatics is cheap. It requires no materials to speak of. All one needs is a space (most libraries have meeting or multi-purpose rooms that would serve well), the idea or story (certainly the shelves of the library are loaded with ideas and stories), the children, and a leader. Creative dramatics is certainly cheaper and less worrisome than producing a play; one is spared the expense of scripts, props, costumes, and scenery. Perhaps most important though, creative dramatics adapts well to the time allotted for programs in the library and it allows for a certain attrition rate in the children. You never have to worry if someone drops out; all the children can play any of the parts.

Because creative dramatics is strongly linked to stories, it is linked to books and this, I believe, is the best reason for including it as a library program. In our classes at the library, Mrs. Reed and I cooperated in putting out book displays related to the particular sessions. The children were encouraged to check out books having something to do with our stories. Statistics on creative dramatics and its relationship to reading are limited, but from our experience I would say that there is a correlation. Perhaps creative dramatics does not make the children better readers, but I believe it is a way of bringing reluctant children to books.

Because this would be an experimental venture, we decided to keep the program modest. We began in late September and scheduled only six classes for the semester. The first five met every other Saturday morning. The last session was just prior to Christmas and was a combination creative dramatics presentation (with parents invited) and Christmas Party. For the second semester we followed the same format—ending with a combination creative dramatics presentation and Easter Egg Hunt just before Easter

---

Report on the PLSC/JMRT/VLA Survey on Children's Programs in Public Libraries in Virginia and in the Greater Washington Area, Winter, 1973.

Sunday. The classes met for 45 minutes to an hour, a good time limit especially when dealing with younger children.

Exactly what happens in a creative dramatics class? Like its definition, this too varies greatly. As in a story hour, the session is often organized around a favorite story or poem. Unlike a story hour, more activities lead up to the introduction of the story. Techniques differ from one creative dramatics leader to another, but in my case I like to begin with simple movement exercises to relax the children, proceed to a short discussion in which questions lead the children to try to guess what the story for the day might be about. Then, I use what I call my Magic Clue Box (a cardboard box painted and decorated to resemble an old chest). The box opens with a Magic Key and inside is something to help the children guess what the story might be. The story is then presented to the children and we go on to plan and play it. The acting is of an improvisational nature with the children alternating the various roles in the story with each playing. The leader directs the children to more honest playing and encourages constructive criticism from the class after each playing. Each child is given a chance to attempt different roles, but no children are forced to play; a creative dramatics class is part audience too.

A mention of the stories used should be made. At Duncan we worked with *The Three Billie Goats Gruff, Little Miss Muffet, Peter Rabbit, The Adventure of the Three Little Rabbits, Caps for Sale, The Snowman,* and *The Monkey and the Peddler*—all stories familiar to children's librarians. It is best to choose stories with a strong conflict, and children, especially at this younger age, respond well to characters very different from themselves. (The Troll in *Three Billy Goats Gruff* is especially popular.)

Mrs. Reed and I were pleased with our program. We began the first semester with a total of twelve children enrolled, of which ten came regularly. Second semester, the word had spread and we had twenty-two names on our list. Of these sixteen or seventeen came regularly; this is really the maximum number for a creative dramatics class especially with younger children. A certain amount of attrition is to be expected. Some children simply do not respond to creative dramatics, sometimes families are out of town, sometimes the lure of Saturday morning cartoons is too much. But the enthusiasm was there and the classes definitely survived.

I am, firstly, a drama teacher and as such I am interested in fostering the cause of drama. It is natural then that I would support a creative dramatics program for the libraries. However, I am not alone in this support. In the Washington area both the Montgomery County Library and the Prince George's Memorial County Library are offering creative dramatics classes to their juvenile patrons. The Arlington County Public Library has experimented with creative dramatics classes recently as have the

McIntire Public Library in Charlottesville and the Henrico County Public Library in Richmond. Experiences differ from library to library, but most children's librarians were enthusiastic about the possibilities of these programs.

My practical proposal then is that you give creative dramatics a try. Any children's librarian who is comfortable handling a story hour group can most probably learn, and come to enjoy, leading a creative dramatics class. Books on the subject are readily available. Look around your community; chances are you'll find someone with a background in drama who would be very happy to help with a creative dramatics class. Check classes offered by local colleges and universities; creative dramatics is becoming a frequent offering.

Creative dramatics can have many benefits to the children who participate. The program can put you in touch with many mothers in the community and be a great public relations draw for the library. The sessions can bring new people, both children and adults, into the library and acquaint them with books. A program is easily started as an offshoot of an already functioning story hour. I hope you will consider creative dramatics as a juvenile program in your library. I know you'll be as pleased as Stella and I were with the enthusiastic reception creative dramatics had in Alexandria.

The Media Specialist and Dramatic Productions

by Celestine Bloomfield

Anyone can produce fantastic professional plays, operettas, P.T.A. programs and holiday pageants. Many media specialists find themselves
responsible for school plays. Drama should be fun for students and sponsors
alike; by sharing duties, teachers and media specialists can present a
dazzling production with a minimum of difficulty.

The media specialist's role may range from procurer of plays and
writer of scripts to official researcher and historian. S/he may help to locate
materials for production and keep the set and props historically accurate.
For the media specialist who finds her/himself solely responsible for a
theatrical production, here are a few helpful suggestions.

Execute utmost caution when choosing the script.

1. Examine the cast members for the number of characters and the gender
   of the characters and note which characters can be changed, expanded or
   deleted.
2. Check the set for feasibility. Anticipate scene changes and construction
   problems. Sets can be simplified and range in complexity from brown
   paper murals and cardboard boxes to overstuffed chairs and sofas
   purloined from home.
3. Props are very important and usually very easy to construct if not readily
   available. While doing a Roman play, we made the soldiers' helmets by
   using a safety hard hat as a base for the paper mache helmets. The
   helmets were then painted and decorated.
4. Bow to the music teacher's decision when it comes to musicals and
   operettas. She knows how difficult the songs will be to learn and the
   pupils' ability to handle them. Non-musical productions flow more
   smoothly with the added touch of music before the show as the audience
   enters and during intermission and curtain calls.

5. Costumes can be as elaborate as desired. Remember the time and costs involved and consider which method will be used to obtain costumes. Look around for talented co-workers and parents. Fabric for costumes can not always be purchased so consider using crepe paper, cardboard, old towels, sheets and clothes.

6. Make-up is fun and is the final touch for characterization. Basic make-up supplies can be begged, bought or created. Lots of ladies have make-up and wigs that they never use and really don't want. Ask for donations. Commercial greasepaints are great to have but you can make your own by using shortening. Irene Corey, a Dallas make-up artist, includes recipes for greasepaint in the October 18, 1977 issue of *Woman's Day*. Look in your yellow pages under theatrical supplies or costumes for places to buy make-up and keep a list of current prices.

Keep a handy file loaded with play suggestions and sources. Back issues of magazines such as *Plays* and *Instructor* provide excellent seasonal material. Collect poems for special occasions and use them as filler if you must adapt a play or invent a script. Expose students to plays by reading aloud. Play original cast recordings of Broadway musicals. Lend a helping hand and an ear when students write their own plays.

Not all media specialists produce plays, however, most do use dramatics. Any good storyteller is highly skilled so don't be afraid to branch out. Have you ever had your pupils act out a story after it has been read? They enjoy it and it tests their retention as well. With older students, try to adapt short stories or novels into plays and skits. Langston Hughes, and Jess B. Simple's stories are easy to adapt and students love them.

Drama is merely another tool to use in educating our children. A media specialist should be prepared to serve the teacher as dramatist equally as well as math teacher, the gym teacher, and the special education teacher. Dramatics present yet another opportunity for media specialists to work within the school's total curriculum.

REFERENCES

Alexander, Sue. *Small Plays for Special Days*. New York: Seabury Press, 1977.

Barwell, Eve. *Disguises You Can Make*. New York: Lothrop, Lee & Shepard Company, 1977.

Eisner, Viviene. *Quick and Easy Holiday Costumes*. New York: Lothrop, Lee & Shepard Company, 1977.

"Halloween Greasepaint" *Woman's Day*, October 18, 1977, p. 120.

"Not on Every Bush"

by Sarah Yoder Scott

One blustery day in March, I gathered my second graders around me and read Marcia Brown's version of an old French folktale, *Stone Soup*. "Children," I asked quietly, "do you think we could make a play out of this story?"

"Yes, yes," came a chorus of excited voices.

Earlier in the school year we had done a few short plays—informal, spontaneous responses to stories. Now, it seemed the children were ready for a full-scale, formal production.

During the next few weeks, I reread the story daily and we discussed it from various points of view—French peasant life in "olden" times, things needed on stage, and different emotions shown in various parts of the story. One day we all sat in a circle on the stage and tried to express on our faces feelings of fatigue, fear, surprise, dismay, amazement, and so on, as the story was read.

On other days at the AV Center, small groups took turns viewing filmstrips, listening to records, assimilating more and more *Stone Soup*. Soon most everyone had the whole story memorized.

The filmstrip of the story served another purpose. By mounting a large sheet of art paper on the easel and getting the projector at the proper distance, the different scenes could be traced and later painted. Then, sprawled on the floor with wide-lined writing paper, felt pen in hand, each child copied the lines to accompany his picture. "Be sure to spell all words correctly and put in punctuation marks. Watch for 'talking marks' in the story," I reminded them. When all forty-three pictures and the accompanying text were completed, they were placed in the corridor. Pupils from other classes stopped to look and read.

Quotations from the story began to appear in the children's formal conversation. "Such men don't grow on every bush" and "fancy that" were favorites.

The getting-acquainted stage over, it was time to begin formal rehearsals. Parts were assigned. No one was left out. Each child had his own copy of the script. However, I soon discovered that it was best to leave it behind and come to the stage empty-handed.

The most difficult task for the children was learning the correct movements to synchronize with their speaking. In their nervousness they crowded together, stood in front of each other, and lost their conversational thread.

But just when things bogged down and I felt ready to "throw the whole play out the window," the kindergarten teacher came to our rescue. She offered many helpful, practical suggestions, such as marking the stage place for each character with small pieces of masking tape, marking the places for stage properties, and working with small groups on stage in the morning before the bell rang.

But we were still working with brown cardboard furniture boxes for village houses and ordinary overhead lighting. At this point a fifth- and sixth-grade class with their teacher went into action. For more than a week we continued practicing our lines in the classroom while these marvelous people took over the stage set and costume making and lighting. Several other pupils helped the second graders practice their lines. No careless speech was permitted.

The speech teacher had given some help on this earlier. During a regularly scheduled therapy period for one of my pupils, she had invited the class to the auditorium. How we laughed as the children took turns on stage. The teacher whispered some words into a child's ear as he stood with his back to the audience. He then said the words aloud, while other children responded from the far side of the room, repeating what they had heard. When "I'm going to hit you" was understood as "I'm gonna eat ya," they saw clearly the need for correct pronunciation, enunciation, projection, and speaking pace.

Our music teacher used part of the scheduled music periods to teach a lovely little dance needed for the play.

At last the stage was finished and two older boys stood ready to operate the light switch. The effect of beautiful scenery and colored lights was magic. The children seemed transported from the real to the imaginary world of French peasants and soldiers.

The following days ran smoothly. All that remained were polishing certain parts and writing letters of invitation to parents and friends. The day our scheduled performance arrived so did a blizzard. Therefore, we had to postpone the show, but it made little difference. We turned out a beautiful performance.

When the last bit of straw was swept from the floor, the costumes folded and put away, and I had time for coffee breaks, it was time to sit back and ask, "What has been accomplished?"

The fifth- and sixth-grade teacher approached the problem directly with her students. She asked response to the following:

1. List two or three things you have learned.
2. Explain what effect lighting has on a play.
3. How do costumes help portray character?
4. Give three rules to follow in regard to the speaking roles.

Here are some responses:

"We divided into committees and we learned to work together without fooling round."

"Lighting makes the play more interesting."

"Costumes and makeup help you see the people as they are."

"With the little children, you have to stay on a line until they say it right."

When I put the problem to the second graders, they enthusiastically responded.

"You have to keep in the play and pay attention all the time or your face looks dull."

"You must get all sounds in the words and talk loud."

When we returned to our normal routine, the children's ability to read had improved.

Many times I asked myself, "How and why did I get into this?" But when the big yellow buses delivered the youngsters, all fresh and bright-eyed, I met them gladly and we adventured together into another day.

Here is the recipe for those who may wish to experiment:

Twenty-four or more energetic second graders, one ordinary teacher, an understanding and supporting principal, an assortment of wonderful, talented coworkers, and one older class and their teacher, willing to help.

Season with generous portions of hard work, enthusiasm, and good humor. Simmer six to eight weeks but watch that it doesn't boil over. When ready, let starry-eyed youngsters serve to a spellbound audience. *"Such children don't grow on every bush."*

Additional Resources

American Alliance for Health, Physical Education, Recreation, and Dance. "Creative Dramatics." *Practical Pointers* 1 (September 1977): 1–9.
> Provides experiences and a wide variety of activities for all age groups and ability levels.

The Arts, Education, and Americans Panel. *Coming to Our Senses: The Significance of the Arts for American Education.* New York: McGraw-Hill, 1977.
> Explains, in the constant theme throughout the book, the importance of the integration of the arts into other curricular areas in education.

Batinich, Mary Ellen. "Curtain Going Up." *Language Arts* 52 (September 1975): 836–38.
> Describes materials designed to stimulate students and to teach creative expression.

Berger, Allen, and Smith, Blanche Hope. *Language Activities.* Urbana, IL: National Council of Teachers of English, 1973.
> Relates specifically to materials for teaching communication skills and literature.

Bressler, Jean, and Johnson, Eileen. "The 'What Else' of Poetry Dramatization." *Media & Methods* 14 (April 1978): 75–77.
> Includes recommendations for adding music, mime, visuals, etc. to poetry reading.

Chambers, Dewey W. "Children's Literature and the Allied Arts." *Elementary English* 48 (October 1971): 622–27.
> Discusses ways to encourage talented children through the medium of literature.

Chesler, Mark, and Fox, Robert. *Role-Playing Methods in the Classroom.* Chicago, IL: Science Research Associates, 1966.
> Describes the techniques and preparations required for using role-playing.

Drutcher, Frances. "Let Them Live Those Rhymes!" *Instructor* 85 (March 1976): 109.

> Discusses the use of imagination to provide a stimulus for teaching nursery rhymes.

Duke, Charles R. *Creative Dramatics and English Teaching*. Urbana, IL: National Council of Teachers of English, 1973.

> Explains sequencing and methods for applications of creative dramatics.

Ehrlich, Harriet W. "Creative Dramatics as a Classroom Teaching Technique." *Elementary English* 51 (January 1974): 75–80.

> Describes dramatization as both a cognitive and resourceful teaching tool.

Ellis, Helene. "Step into Another's Shoes." *Instructor* 83 (May 1974): 82.

> Relates situation activities which help students broaden their outlooks about skills in everyday life.

Feinberg, Rose M. "Creative Drama Needs a Building Process." *Language Arts* 53 (February 1976): 184–86.

> Explores the 5 stages necessary for building a creative program of dramatization which will help students attain positive feelings about themselves and others.

Furner, Beatrice. "Creative Writing through Creative Dramatics." *Elementary English* 50 (March 1973): 405–08, 416.

> Explains how sensory awareness provides motivation for nondirected writing experiences.

Grasty, Patricia E. "Creative Dramatics: No Age Limit." *Elementary English* 51 (January 1974): 72–73.

> Discusses the ways that effective teacher training in dramatization produces not only new techniques, but also a new understanding and appreciation.

Hardy, Sister Marie Paula. "Drama in the Classroom." *Elementary English* 51 (January 1974): 94–102.

> Describes the role of the teacher in organizing, suggesting, guiding, and planning experiences in dramatization for children.

Hayes, Eloise. "Drama is English in Action." *Language Arts* 53 (Fall 1976): 179–83.

> By creating excitement in the classroom, dramatization strengthens oral and written language, reading, and creative writing.

Jackson, Walt, and Musil, Lew. "Becoming a Concrete Poem." *Language Arts* 54 (March 1977): 290–93.

> Describes how students added a creative dimension to writing poetry by turning their concrete poems into performances.

Lewis, Nev. "Speakeasy: Using Speech and Drama in the Library."
Assistant Librarian 69 (July–August 1976): 131–33.
> Through dramatization, explains how the library can be promoted as an
> entertaining as well as interesting place.

McCaslin, Nellie, ed. *Children and Drama*. New York: McKay, 1975.
> Records thoughts and reactions to creative drama both personally and edu-
> cationally.

McGregor, Marjorie. "Cognitive Development through Creative Dramatics." *Speech Teacher* 22 (September 1973): 220–25.
> Discusses dramatization and its contribution to the development of vocabu-
> lary, differentiation, concept formation, etc.

Madeja, Stanley. *All the Arts for Every Child*. St. Louis, MO: Central
Midwest Regional Educational Laboratory, 1973.
> Gives final reports on the Arts in General Education Project in the school
> district of University City, Missouri. Presents mini-introductions to cultural
> studies, instruction in the creative process, and cultural appreciation.

Madeja, Stanley. *Through the Arts to the Aesthetic*. St. Louis, MO: Central
Midwest Regional Educational Laboratory, 1978.
> Describes, in 44 units of the elementary curriculum, the uses of aesthetic
> education for all art forms, including literature, film, music, dance, visual
> arts, and theater. The units integrate the aesthetic into the subject matter in an
> area of study.

Marcous, J. Paul. "Helping Emotionally Disturbed Children through Creative Dramatics." *Communication Education* 25 (March 1976): 174–77.
> Cites opportunities presented by dramatization from behavioral, communi-
> cational, and creative standpoints.

Mazor, Rickey. "Drama as Experience." *Language Arts* 55 (March 1978):
328–33.
> Using dramatization as a structure to provide experiences to express a child's
> uniqueness promotes creativity and reduces destructiveness.

Moffeet, James. *Drama: What Is Happening?* Urbana, IL: National
Council of Teachers of English, 1967.
> Discusses teaching methods relating to dialogue, soliloquy, monologue,
> style, etc.

Oliver, Linda. "Development of Young Children's Dramatic and Public
Speaking Skills." *The Elementary School Journal* 73 (November 1972):
95–100.
> Gives the results of a study which involved the development of a sequenced
> program in public speaking and dramatics with kindergarten and first-grade
> students.

Reed, Linda. "Creative Drama in the Language Arts Program, or 'Catch that crab before he finds a hole!' " *Elementary English* 51 (January 1974): 103–10.
> Describes ERIC documents relating to dramatization.

Rice, Dale R., and Sisk, Preston F. "Teaching Elementary Science through Creative Dramatics." *School Science and Mathematics* 80 (January 1980): 61–64.
> Shows that relating intellectual scientific content to personal feelings provides expanded experiences in the subject matter.

Shuman, R. Baird. *Educational Drama for Today's Schools*. Metuchen, NJ: Scarecrow Press, 1978.
> Discusses educational drama in broad concepts relating to values, language development, and the creative process.

Stewig, John Warren. "Instructional Strategies." *Elementary English* 50 (March 1973): 393–96, 413.
> Uses pictures as the departure point for developing skills in creative dramatics and language development.

Thacker, Linda. "Teach Reading through Dramatics." *School and Community* 61 (March 1975): 32.
> Provides precise instructions for utilizing drama in the classroom.

Thurman, Evelyn. "Creative Dramatics: Don't Miss the Fun." *Catholic Library World* 49 (October 1977): 120–23.
> A librarian shares her successful adventures using dramatized stories with children.

Via, Richard A. "Participatory English: Drama." *Language Arts* 53 (Fall 1976): 175–78.
> Explores dramatization and improvisation as ways to stimulate vocabulary growth and development.

Walker, T. A. "Language through Drama." *English Language Teacher Journal* 31 (January 1977): 141–45.
> Discusses the limitations and functions of using improvisation in the classroom.

Ward, Fred. "A Day on the Downs." *London Times Educational Supplement* 3213 (December 31, 1976): 10–11.
> Recounts a drama project of recreating the Roman occupation of Britain with 200 school children.

Wright, Lin. "Creative Dramatics and the Development of Role-taking in the Elementary Classroom." *Elementary English* 51 (January 1974): 89–93, 131.
> Discusses whether dramatization can help to improve children's skills in role-taking and, if it does, which activities best promote this development.

Index

Compiled by Linda Schexnaydre

12, 15–16, 19, 21, 29–32,
33–41, 77, 102–04, 120, 130,
138, 152, 163, 168, 207, 209,
213, 214
Emotionally disturbed children, 194–
95, 213
English. *See* Children's literature;
Language development; Litera-
ture; Novels; Poetry; Stories to
dramatize.
Environmental studies, 147, 148–56
Ethnic groups, 16, 19–20
Exceptional children, 15, 175, 176–
77, 183–96
Explorers, 130–37
Extrapolation, 77, 81–82

Fables, 5, 79
Fairy tales, 34–35, 37, 82
Fiction. *See* Children's literature;
Novels; Stories to dramatize.
Folktales, 207–09
Foreign languages, 59

Gaming, 147, 148–56, 159
Gifted students, 15, 175, 183–88
Group social skills, 22, 66, 89, 176–
77

Handicapped students, 15, 175,
176–77, 183–96
High school students, 8, 11, 12, 18–
22, 42, 78, 97
History, 11, 16, 119, 120–37, 165,
167, 175, 180–82, 214
Humor, 147, 157–59

Imagination, 14, 15, 31, 63, 89–90,
169
Improvisation, 4, 10, 17, 19, 20, 30–
31, 33–35, 77, 80–81, 88,
94–95, 190, 200, 203, 214
Indians. *See* American Indians.

Junior high school students, 7–8,
18–19, 21–22, 62, 78, 97, 138,
141, 152

Kindergarten students, 19, 53, 213

Language arts. *See* Literature; Oral
communication skills; Reading;
Vocabulary building; Writing
skills.
Language development, 9, 18–20,
22, 30, 32, 33–41, 44–45,
68–73, 136, 169, 189, 191, 194,
201
Learning disabled students, 175, 176,
183–88, 189, 190–91, 194
Lewis and Clark expedition, 131–35
Library programs, 199–209, 213, 214
Listening skills, 39, 53, 66, 70, 189,
194
Literature, 11, 20–21, 22, 35, 77,
78–84, 170. *See also* Children's
literature; Novels; Poetry; Stories
to dramatize.
Low-ability students, 19, 21, 28, 62–
63, 66, 191

Media specialists, 199, 205–06
Mentally handicapped children,
191–92
Minority students, 16, 19–20
Moral development, 119, 138–40
Movement, 16, 19, 37–38, 70,
95–96, 190, 192, 193, 194
Music, 31, 141–43, 157–59, 164,
190, 192, 193, 195, 205, 208
Mythology, 78, 81, 87

News broadcasts, 147, 157–59
Novels, 78, 82, 83, 142–43. *See also*
Stories to dramatize.
Nursery rhymes, 55, 212
Nutrition, 147, 157–59

Observation skills, 93
Oral communication skills, 19, 22,
36, 53, 55, 95–96, 189

Pantomime, 4, 9, 16, 19, 28, 30, 31,
52, 68, 77, 79–80, 89, 90, 91,
171, 190, 192, 193, 194, 200
Parent involvement, 201–02